# HISTORY & GEOGRAPHY 300
## Teacher's Guide

**Author:**
Rachelle Wiersma, M.A.

**Editor:**
Laura Messner

**Managing Editor:**
Alan Christopherson, M.S.

**Media Credits:**
**Page 106:** © Tigatelu, iStock, Thinkstock

All maps are © Image Resources unless otherwise stated.

**804 N. 2nd Ave. E.**
**Rock Rapids, IA 51246-1759**

# HISTORY & GEOGRAPHY 300

LIFEPAC® Overview

# HISTORY & GEOGRAPHY SCOPE & SEQUENCE

| | Your World (Grade 1) | U.S. History (Grade 2) | U.S. Geography and History (Grade 3) |
|---|---|---|---|
| **Unit 1** | I AM A SPECIAL PERSON<br>• God made me<br>• You are God's child<br>• All about you<br>• Using proper manners | LOOKING BACK<br>Remembering last year<br>Learning about early times<br>The trail of the Native Americans<br>Symbols and historic places | U.S. GEOGRAPHY AND HISTORY STUDY SKILLS<br>• Map skills<br>• Resources<br>• Community |
| **Unit 2** | LET'S COMMUNICATE<br>• Sounds people make<br>• Sounds that communicate<br>• Communicating without sound<br>• Communicating with God | SETTLING THE NEW WORLD<br>The first settlers<br>Colonies of the new world<br>War for Independence<br>Symbols and historical places | NEW ENGLAND STATES<br>• ME, NH, VT, MA, RI, and CT<br>• New England geography<br>• New England resources<br>• New England community |
| **Unit 3** | I HAVE FEELINGS<br>• I feel sad<br>• I feel afraid<br>• I feel happy<br>• I have other feelings | A NEW GOVERNMENT FOR A NEW COUNTRY<br>A study of government<br>Creating a government<br>Our government<br>Symbols and historical places | MID-ATLANTIC STATES<br>• NY, PA, NJ, DE, MD, and DC<br>• Mid-Atlantic geography<br>• Mid-Atlantic resources<br>• Mid-Atlantic community |
| **Unit 4** | I LIVE IN A FAMILY<br>• My mother and father<br>• My brothers and sisters<br>• My grandparents<br>• What my family does | GOVERNMENT UNDER THE CONSTITUTION<br>Article One – The Legislative Branch<br>Article Two – The Executive Branch<br>Article Three – The Judicial Branch<br>The Bill of Rights – Symbols and historical places | SOUTHERN-ATLANTIC STATES<br>• WV, VA, NC, SC, GA, and FL<br>• Southern Atlantic geography<br>• Southern Atlantic resources<br>• Southern Atlantic community |
| **Unit 5** | YOU BELONG TO FAMILIES<br>• Getting ready in the morning<br>• Walking to school<br>• The school family<br>• The church family | OUR GOVERNMENT CLOSE TO HOME<br>Our state governments<br>Our local governments<br>Citizens of the United States<br>Symbols and historical places | SOUTHERN STATES<br>• KY, TN, MS, LA, AL, OK, TX, and AR<br>• Southern geography<br>• Southern resources<br>• Southern community |
| **Unit 6** | PLACES PEOPLE LIVE<br>• Life on the farm<br>• Life in the city<br>• Life by the sea | WESTWARD – FROM THE ORIGINAL COLONIES<br>The United States grows<br>The Lewis and Clark Expedition<br>The Old Southwest<br>Symbols and historical places | GREAT LAKES STATES<br>• OH, IN, IL, MI, WI, and MN<br>• Great Lakes geography<br>• Great Lakes resources<br>• Great Lakes community |
| **Unit 7** | COMMUNITY HELPERS<br>• Firefighters and police officers<br>• Doctors<br>• City workers<br>• Teachers and ministers | SETTLING THE FRONTIER<br>The Texas frontier<br>Westward expansion<br>Meet America's pioneers<br>Symbols and historical places | MIDWESTERN STATES<br>• ND, SD, NE, KS, MO, and IA<br>• Midwestern geography<br>• Midwestern resources<br>• Midwestern community |
| **Unit 8** | I LOVE MY COUNTRY<br>• America discovered<br>• The Pilgrims<br>• The United States begins<br>• Respect for your country | EXPLORING AMERICA WITH MAPS<br>Directions on a map<br>Reading roads and symbols<br>Natural features<br>Symbols and historical places | MOUNTAIN STATES<br>• MT, ID, WY, NV, UT, CO, AZ, and NM<br>• Mountain geography<br>• Mountain resources<br>• Mountain community |
| **Unit 9** | I LIVE IN THE WORLD<br>• The globe<br>• Countries<br>• Friends in Mexico<br>• Friends in Japan | PAST, PRESENT, AND FUTURE MAPS<br>City maps<br>Building maps<br>History of maps<br>Symbols and historical places | PACIFIC STATES<br>• WA, OR, CA, AK, and HI<br>• Pacific geography<br>• Pacific resources<br>• Pacific community |
| **Unit 10** | THE WORLD AND YOU<br>• You are special<br>• Your family<br>• Your school and church<br>• Your world | REVIEW UNITED STATES HISTORY<br>The United States begins<br>Creating a government<br>Mapping the United States | U.S. GEOGRAPHY AND HISTORY REVIEW<br>• U.S. geographical features<br>• Eastern U.S. review<br>• Western U.S. review |

# HISTORY & GEOGRAPHY SCOPE & SEQUENCE

| World Geography and Culture (Grade 4) | U.S. History (Grade 5) | Civilizations (Grade 6) | |
|---|---|---|---|
| **OUR EARTH**<br>• The surface of the Earth<br>• Early explorations of the Earth<br>• Exploring from space<br>• Exploring the oceans | **A NEW WORLD**<br>• Exploration of America<br>• The first colonies<br>• Conflict with Britain<br>• Birth of the United States | **WORLD GEOGRAPHY**<br>• Latitude and longitude<br>• Western and eastern hemispheres<br>• The southern hemisphere<br>• Political and cultural regions | Unit 1 |
| **SEAPORT CITIES**<br>• Sydney<br>• Hong Kong<br>• Istanbul<br>• London | **A NEW NATION**<br>• War for Independence<br>• Life in America<br>• A new form of government<br>• The nation's early years | **THE CRADLE OF CIVILIZATION**<br>• Mesopotamia<br>• The land of Israel<br>• The nation of Israel<br>• Egypt | Unit 2 |
| **DESERT LANDS**<br>• What is a desert?<br>• Where are the deserts?<br>• How do people live in the desert? | **A TIME OF TESTING**<br>• Louisiana Purchase<br>• War of 1812<br>• Sectionalism<br>• Improvements in trade and travel | **THE CIVILIZATIONS OF GREECE AND ROME**<br>• Geography of the region<br>• Beginning civilizations<br>• Contributions to other civilizations<br>• The influence of Christianity | Unit 3 |
| **GRASSLANDS**<br>• Grasslands of the world<br>• Ukraine<br>• Kenya<br>• Argentina | **A GROWING NATION**<br>• Andrew Jackson's influence<br>• Texas and Oregon<br>• Mexican War<br>• The nation divides | **LIFE IN THE MIDDLE AGES**<br>• The feudal system<br>• Books and schools<br>• The Crusades<br>• Trade and architecture | Unit 4 |
| **TROPICAL RAINFORESTS**<br>• Facts about rainforests<br>• Rainforests of the world<br>• The Amazon rainforest<br>• The Congo rainforest | **A DIVIDED NATION**<br>• Civil War<br>• Reconstruction<br>• Gilded Age<br>• The need for reform | **SIX SOUTH AMERICAN COUNTRIES**<br>• Brazil<br>• Colombia<br>• Venezuela<br>• Three Guianas | Unit 5 |
| **THE POLAR REGIONS**<br>• The polar regions: coldest places in the world<br>• The Arctic polar region<br>• The Antarctic polar region | **A CHANGING NATION**<br>• Progressive reforms<br>• Spanish-American War<br>• World War I<br>• Roaring Twenties | **OTHER SOUTH AMERICAN COUNTRIES**<br>• Ecuador and Peru<br>• Bolivia and Uruguay<br>• Paraguay and Argentina<br>• Chile | Unit 6 |
| **MOUNTAIN COUNTRIES**<br>• Peru — the Andes<br>• The Incas and modern Peru<br>• Nepal — the Himalayas<br>• Switzerland — the Alps | **DEPRESSION AND WAR**<br>• The Great Depression<br>• War begins in Europe<br>• War in Europe<br>• War in the Pacific | **AFRICA**<br>• Geography and cultures<br>• Countries of northern Africa<br>• Countries of central Africa<br>• Countries of southern Africa | Unit 7 |
| **ISLAND COUNTRIES**<br>• Islands of the Earth<br>• Cuba<br>• Iceland<br>• Japan | **COLD WAR**<br>• Korean War and other crises<br>• Vietnam War<br>• Civil Rights movement<br>• Upheaval in America | **MODERN WESTERN EUROPE**<br>• The Renaissance<br>• The Industrial Revolution<br>• World War I<br>• World War II | Unit 8 |
| **NORTH AMERICA**<br>• Geography<br>• Lands, lakes, and rivers<br>• Northern countries<br>• Southern countries | **INTO THE NEW MILLENNIUM**<br>• Watergate and détente<br>• The fall of communism<br>• The Persian Gulf<br>• Issues of the new millennium | **MODERN EASTERN EUROPE**<br>• Early government<br>• Early churches<br>• Early countries<br>• Modern countries | Unit 9 |
| **OUR WORLD IN REVIEW**<br>• Europe and the explorers<br>• Asia and Africa<br>• Southern continents<br>• North America and the North Pole | **THE UNITED STATES OF AMERICA**<br>• Beginning America until 1830<br>• Stronger America 1830-1930<br>• 1930 to the end of the millennium<br>• The new millennium | **DEVELOPMENT OF OUR WORLD**<br>• Cradle of civilization<br>• The Middle Ages<br>• Modern Europe<br>• South America and Africa | Unit 10 |

# HISTORY & GEOGRAPHY SCOPE & SEQUENCE

| | Anthropology, Sociology, Economics, and State History (Grade 7) | U.S. History (Grade 8) | Civics and World Geography (Grade 9) |
|---|---|---|---|
| Unit 1 | WHAT IS HISTORY?<br>• Definition and significance of history<br>• Historians and the historical method<br>• Views of history | EUROPE COMES TO AMERICA<br>• Voyages of Columbus<br>• Spanish exploration<br>• Other exploration<br>• The first colonies | HERITAGE OF THE UNITED STATES<br>• American colonies<br>• Acquisitions and annexations<br>• Backgrounds to freedom<br>• Backgrounds to society |
| Unit 2 | WHAT IS GEOGRAPHY?<br>• Classes of geography<br>• Geography and relief of the Earth<br>• Maps and the study of our world<br>• Time zones | BRITISH AMERICA<br>• English colonies<br>• Government<br>• Lifestyle<br>• Wars with France | OUR NATIONAL GOVERNMENT<br>• Ideals of national government<br>• National government developed<br>• Legislative and executive branches<br>• Judicial branch |
| Unit 3 | U.S. HISTORY AND GEOGRAPHY<br>• Geography of the United States<br>• Early history of the United States<br>• Physical regions of the United States<br>• Cultural regions of the United States | THE AMERICAN REVOLUTION<br>• British control<br>• Rebellion of the colonies<br>• War for independence<br>• Constitution | STATE AND LOCAL GOVERNMENT<br>• Powers of state government<br>• County government<br>• Township government<br>• City government |
| Unit 4 | ANTHROPOLOGY<br>• Understanding anthropology<br>• The unity of people<br>• The diversity of people<br>• The culture of people groups | A FIRM FOUNDATION<br>• Washington's presidency<br>• Adams' administration<br>• Jeffersonian Democracy<br>• War of 1812 | PLANNING A CAREER<br>• Definition of a career<br>• God's will concerning a career<br>• Selecting a career<br>• Preparation for a career |
| Unit 5 | SOCIOLOGY — PEOPLE IN GROUPS<br>• Sociology defined<br>• Historical development<br>• Importance to Christians<br>• Method of sociology | A GROWING NATION<br>• Jacksonian Era<br>• Northern border<br>• Southern border<br>• Industrial Revolution | CITIZENSHIP<br>• Citizenship defined<br>• Gaining citizenship<br>• Rights of citizenship<br>• Responsibilities of citizenship |
| Unit 6 | U.S. ANTHROPOLOGY AND SOCIOLOGY<br>• Cultural background of the United States<br>• Native American cultures<br>• Cultures from distant lands<br>• Cultural and social interaction | THE CIVIL WAR<br>• Division and secession<br>• Civil War<br>• Death of Lincoln<br>• Reconstruction | THE EARTH AND MAN<br>• Man inhabits the Earth<br>• Man's home on the Earth<br>• Man develops the Earth<br>• The future of the Earth |
| Unit 7 | ECONOMICS — RESOURCES AND NEED<br>• Economics defined<br>• Methods of the economist<br>• Tools of the economist<br>• An experiment in economy | GILDED AGE TO PROGRESSIVE ERA<br>• Rise of industry<br>• Wild West<br>• America as a world power<br>• Progressive era | REGIONS OF THE WORLD<br>• A region defined<br>• Geographic and climate regions<br>• Cultural and political regions<br>• Economic regions of Europe |
| Unit 8 | POLITICAL SCIENCE<br>• Definition of political science<br>• Roots of Western thought<br>• Modern political thinkers<br>• Political theory | A WORLD IN CONFLICT<br>• World War I<br>• Great Depression<br>• New Deal<br>• World War II | MAN AND HIS ENVIRONMENT<br>• The physical environment<br>• Drug abuse<br>• The social environment<br>• Man's responsibilities |
| Unit 9 | STATE ECONOMICS AND POLITICS<br>• Background of state government<br>• State government<br>• State finance<br>• State politics | COLD WAR AMERICA<br>• Origins of the Cold War<br>• Vietnam<br>• Truman to Nixon<br>• Ending of the Cold War | TOOLS OF THE GEOGRAPHER<br>• The globe<br>• Types of maps<br>• Reading maps<br>• The Earth in symbol form |
| Unit 10 | SOCIAL SCIENCES REVIEW<br>• History and geography<br>• Anthropology<br>• Sociology<br>• Economics and politics | RECENT AMERICA AND REVIEW<br>• Europe to independence<br>• Colonies to the Civil War<br>• Civil War to World War II<br>• World War II through the Cold War | MAN IN A CHANGING WORLD<br>• Development of the nation<br>• Development of government<br>• Development of the Earth<br>• Solving problems |

# HISTORY & GEOGRAPHY SCOPE & SEQUENCE

| World History (Grade 10) | American History (Grade 11) | Government and Economics (Grade 12) | |
|---|---|---|---|
| **ANCIENT CIVILIZATIONS 1**<br>• Origin of civilization<br>• Early Egypt<br>• Assyria and Babylonia<br>• Persian civilization | **FOUNDATION OF THE REPUBLIC**<br>• Democracy develops<br>• Virginia<br>• New England colonies<br>• Middle and southern colonies | **INTERNATIONAL GOVERNMENTS**<br>• Why have governments?<br>• Types of governments<br>• Governments in our world<br>• Political thinkers | Unit 1 |
| **ANCIENT CIVILIZATIONS 2**<br>• India<br>• China<br>• Greek civilization<br>• Roman Empire | **DEVELOPMENT OF CONSTITUTIONAL GOVERNMENT**<br>• Relations with England<br>• The Revolutionary War<br>• Articles of Confederation<br>• Constitution of the United States | **UNITED STATES GOVERNMENT**<br>• U.S. Constitution<br>• Bill of Rights<br>• Three branches of government<br>• Legislative process | Unit 2 |
| **THE MEDIEVAL WORLD**<br>• Early Middle Ages<br>• Middle Ages in transition<br>• High Middle Ages | **NATIONAL EXPANSION**<br>• A strong federal government<br>• Revolution of 1800<br>• War of 1812<br>• Nationalism and sectionalism | **AMERICAN PARTY SYSTEM**<br>• American party system<br>• Development of political parties<br>• Functions of political parties<br>• Voting | Unit 3 |
| **RENAISSANCE AND REFORMATION**<br>• Changes in government and art<br>• Changes in literature and thought<br>• Advances in science<br>• Reform within the church | **A NATION DIVIDED**<br>• Issues of division<br>• Division of land and people<br>• Economics of slavery<br>• Politics of slavery | **HISTORY OF GOVERNMENTS**<br>• Primitive governments<br>• Beginnings of democracy<br>• Feudalism, theocracy, and democracy<br>• Fascism and Nazism | Unit 4 |
| **GROWTH OF WORLD EMPIRES**<br>• England and France<br>• Portugal and Spain<br>• Austria and Germany<br>• Italy and the Ottoman Empire | **A NATION DIVIDED AND UNITED**<br>• Regionalism<br>• The division<br>• The Civil War<br>• Reconstruction | **THE CHRISTIAN AND GOVERNMENT**<br>• Discrimination and the Christian<br>• Christian attitudes<br>• Public opinion and truth in politics<br>• Politics and propaganda | Unit 5 |
| **THE AGE OF REVOLUTION**<br>• Factors leading to revolution<br>• The English Revolution<br>• The American Revolution<br>• The French Revolution | **U.S. INVOLVEMENT AT HOME AND ABROAD**<br>• Surge of industry<br>• The industrial lifestyle<br>• Isolationism<br>• Involvement in conflict | **FREE ENTERPRISE**<br>• Economics<br>• Competition<br>• Money through history<br>• International finance and currency | Unit 6 |
| **THE INDUSTRIAL REVOLUTION**<br>• Sparks of preparation<br>• Industrial Revolution in England<br>• Industrial Revolution in America<br>• Social changes of the revolution | **THE SEARCH FOR PEACE**<br>• World War I and its aftermath<br>• The Golden Twenties<br>• The Great Depression<br>• The New Deal | **BUSINESS AND YOU**<br>• Running a business<br>• Government and business<br>• Banks and mergers<br>• Deregulation and bankruptcy | Unit 7 |
| **TWO WORLD WARS**<br>• Mounting tension<br>• World War I<br>• Peace and power quests<br>• World War II | **A NATION AT WAR**<br>• Causes of the war<br>• World War II<br>• Korean conflict<br>• Vietnam conflict | **THE STOCK MARKET**<br>• How it started and works<br>• Selecting stocks<br>• Types of stocks<br>• Tracking stocks | Unit 8 |
| **THE 20th CENTURY AFTER 1945**<br>• The Cold War<br>• Korean War and Vietnam War<br>• Collapse of the Soviet Union<br>• The 20th century closes | **CONTEMPORARY AMERICA**<br>• America from 1960 to 2000<br>• International scene from 1960 to 2000<br>• America after 2000<br>• International scene after 2000 | **BUDGET AND FINANCE**<br>• Cash, credit, and checking<br>• Buying a car<br>• Grants, loans, and IRAs<br>• Savings, debit cards, and global currency | Unit 9 |
| **ANCIENT TIMES TO THE 21st CENTURY**<br>• Ancient civilizations<br>• Medieval times<br>• Renaissance and Reformation<br>• Revolutions and Globalization | **UNITED STATES HISTORY**<br>• Basis of democracy<br>• The 1800s<br>• Industrialization<br>• Current history | **GEOGRAPHY**<br>• Euro and International finance<br>• U.S. geography<br>• The global traveler<br>• Neighbors, heroes, and the Holy Land | Unit 10 |

# STRUCTURE OF THE LIFEPAC CURRICULUM

The LIFEPAC curriculum is conveniently structured to provide one Teacher's Guide containing teacher support material with answer keys and ten student worktexts for each subject at grade levels 2 through 12. The worktext format of the LIFEPACs allows the student to read the textual information and complete workbook activities all in the same booklet. The easy-to-follow LIFEPAC numbering system lists the grade as the first number(s) and the last two digits as the number of the series. For example, the Language Arts LIFEPAC at the 6th grade level, 5th book in the series would be LAN0605.

Each LIFEPAC is divided into three to five sections and begins with an introduction or overview of the booklet as well as a series of specific learning objectives to give a purpose to the study of the LIFEPAC. The introduction and objectives are followed by a vocabulary section which may be found at the beginning of each section at the lower levels or in the glossary at the high school level. Vocabulary words are used to develop word recognition and should not be confused with the spelling words introduced later in the LIFEPAC. The student should learn all vocabulary words before working the LIFEPAC sections to improve comprehension, retention, and reading skills.

Each activity or written assignment in grades 2 through 12 has a number for easy identification, such as 1.1. The first number corresponds to the LIFEPAC section and the number to the right of the decimal is the number of the activity.

Teacher checkpoints, which are essential to maintain quality learning, are found at various locations throughout the LIFEPAC.

The teacher should check 1) neatness of work and penmanship, 2) quality of understanding (tested with a short oral quiz), 3) thoroughness of answers (complete sentences and paragraphs, correct spelling, etc.), 4) completion of activities (no blank spaces), and 5) accuracy of answers as compared to the answer key (all answers correct).

The self test questions in grades 2 through 12 are also number coded for easy reference. For example, 2.015 means that this is the 15th question in the self test of Section 2. The first number corresponds to the LIFEPAC section, the zero indicates that it is a self test question, and the number to the right of the zero the question number.

The LIFEPAC test is packaged at the centerfold of each LIFEPAC. It should be removed and put aside before giving the booklet to the student for study.

Answer and test keys in grades 2 through 12 have the same numbering system as the LIFEPACs. The student may be given access to the answer keys (not the test keys) under teacher supervision so that he can score his own work.

A thorough study of the Scope & Sequence by the teacher before instruction begins is essential to the success of the student. The teacher should become familiar with expected skill mastery and understand how these grade-level skills fit into the overall skill development of the curriculum. The teacher should also preview the objectives that appear at the beginning of each LIFEPAC for additional preparation and planning.

# TEST SCORING AND GRADING

Answer keys and test keys give examples of correct answers. They convey the idea, but the student may use many ways to express a correct answer. The teacher should check for the essence of the answer, not for the exact wording. Many questions are high level and require thinking and creativity on the part of the student. Each answer should be scored based on whether or not the main idea written by the student matches the model example. "Any Order" or "Either Order" in a key indicates that no particular order is necessary to be correct.

Most self tests and LIFEPAC tests at the lower elementary levels are scored at 1 point per answer; however, the upper levels may have a point system awarding 2 to 5 points for various answers or questions. Further, the total test points will vary; they may not always equal 100 points. They may be 78, 85, 100, 105, etc.

**Example 1**

**Example 2**

A score box similar to ex. 1 above is located at the end of each self test and on the front of the LIFEPAC test. The bottom score, 72, represents the total number of points possible on the test. The upper score, 58, represents the number of points your student will need to receive an 80% or passing grade. If you wish to establish the exact percentage that your student has achieved, find the total points of his correct answers and divide it by the bottom number (in this case 72). For example, if your student has a point total of 65, divide 65 by 72 for a grade of 90%. Referring to ex. 2, on a test with a total of 105 possible points, the student would have to receive a minimum of 84 correct points for an 80% or passing grade. If your student has received 93 points, simply divide the 93 by 105 for a percentage grade of 89%. Students who receive a score below 80% should review the LIFEPAC and retest using the appropriate Alternate Test found in the Teacher's Guide.

The following is a guideline to assign letter grades for completed LIFEPACs based on a maximum total score of 100 points.

**Example**:

| | | |
|---|---|---|
| LIFEPAC Test | = | 60% of the Total Score (or percent grade) |
| Self Test | = | 25% of the Total Score (average percent of self tests) |
| Reports | = | 10% or 10* points per LIFEPAC |
| Oral Work | = | 5% or 5* points per LIFEPAC |

*Determined by the teacher's subjective evaluation of the student's daily work.

**Example**:

| | | | | | |
|---|---|---|---|---|---|
| LIFEPAC Test Score | = | 92% | $92 \times .60$ | = | 55 points |
| Self Test Average | = | 90% | $90 \times .25$ | = | 23 points |
| Reports | | | | = | 8 points |
| Oral Work | | | | = | 4 points |
| | | | | | |
| TOTAL POINTS | | | | = | 90 points |

**Grade Scale based on point system**:

| | | |
|---|---|---|
| 100 – 94 | = | A |
| 93 – 86 | = | B |
| 85 – 77 | = | C |
| 76 – 70 | = | D |
| Below 70 | = | F |

# TEACHER HINTS AND STUDYING TECHNIQUES

LIFEPAC activities are written to check the level of understanding of the preceding text. The student may look back to the text as necessary to complete these activities; however, a student should never attempt to do the activities without reading (studying) the text first. Self tests and LIFEPAC tests are never open book tests.

Language arts activities (skill integration) often appear within other subject curriculum. The purpose is to give the student an opportunity to test his skill mastery outside of the context in which it was presented.

Writing complete answers (paragraphs) to some questions is an integral part of the LIFEPAC curriculum in all subjects. This builds communication and organization skills, increases understanding and retention of ideas, and helps enforce good penmanship. Complete sentences should be encouraged for this type of activity. Obviously, single words or phrases do not meet the intent of the activity, since multiple lines are given for the response.

Review is essential to student success. Time invested in review where review is suggested will be time saved in correcting errors later. Self tests, unlike the section activities, are closed book. This procedure helps to identify weaknesses before they become too great to overcome. Certain objectives from self tests are cumulative and test previous sections; therefore, good preparation for a self test must include all material studied up to that testing point.

The following procedure checklist has been found to be successful in developing good study habits in the LIFEPAC curriculum.

1. Read the introduction and Table of Contents.
2. Read the objectives.
3. Recite and study the entire vocabulary (glossary) list.
4. Study each section as follows:
   a. Read the introduction and study the section objectives.
   b. Read all the text for the entire section, but answer none of the activities.
   c. Return to the beginning of the section and memorize each vocabulary word and definition.
   d. Reread the section, complete the activities, check the answers with the answer key, correct all errors, and have the teacher check.
   e. Read the self test but do not answer the questions.
   f. Go to the beginning of the first section and reread the text and answers to the activities up to the self test you have not yet done.
   g. Answer the questions to the self test without looking back.
   h. Have the self test checked by the teacher.
   i. Correct the self test and have the teacher check the corrections.
   j. Repeat steps a–i for each section.
5. Use the **SQ3R** method to prepare for the LIFEPAC test.
   **S**can the whole LIFEPAC.
   **Q**uestion yourself on the objectives.
   **R**ead the whole LIFEPAC again.
   **R**ecite through an oral examination.
   **R**eview weak areas.
6. Take the LIFEPAC test as a closed book test.
7. LIFEPAC tests are administered and scored under direct teacher supervision. Students who receive scores below 80% should review the LIFEPAC using the **SQ3R** study method and take the Alternate Test located in the Teacher's Guide. The final test grade may be the grade on the Alternate Test or an average of the grades from the original LIFEPAC test and the Alternate Test.

# GOAL SETTING AND SCHEDULES

Each school must develop its own schedule, because no single set of procedures will fit every situation. The following is an example of a daily schedule that includes the five LIFEPAC subjects as well as time slotted for special activities.

**Possible Daily Schedule**

| | | |
|---|---|---|
| 8:15 – 8:25 | Pledges, prayer, songs, devotions, etc. |
| 8:25 – 9:10 | Bible |
| 9:10 – 9:55 | Language Arts |
| 9:55 – 10:15 | Recess (juice break) |
| 10:15 – 11:00 | Math |
| 11:00 – 11:45 | History & Geography |
| 11:45 – 12:30 | Lunch, recess, quiet time |
| 12:30 – 1:15 | Science |
| 1:15 – | Drill, remedial work, enrichment* |

*****Enrichment**: *Computer time, physical education, field trips, fun reading, games and puzzles, family business, hobbies, resource persons, guests, crafts, creative work, electives, music appreciation, projects.*

Basically, two factors need to be considered when assigning work to a student in the LIFEPAC curriculum.

The first is time. An average of 45 minutes should be devoted to each subject, each day. Remember, this is only an average. Because of extenuating circumstances, a student may spend only 15 minutes on a subject one day and the next day spend 90 minutes on the same subject.

The second factor is the number of pages to be worked in each subject. A single LIFEPAC is designed to take three to four weeks to complete. Allowing about three to four days for LIFEPAC introduction, review, and tests, the student has approximately 15 days to complete the LIFEPAC pages. Simply take the number of pages in the LIFEPAC, divide it by 15 and you will have the number of pages that must be completed on a daily basis to keep the student on schedule. For example, a LIFEPAC containing 45 pages will require three completed pages per day. Again, this is only an average. While working a 45-page LIFEPAC, the student may complete only one page the first day if the text has a lot of activities or reports, but go on to complete five pages the next day.

Long-range planning requires some organization. Because the traditional school year originates in the early fall of one year and continues to late spring of the following year, a calendar should be devised that covers this period of time. Approximate beginning and completion dates can be noted on the calendar as well as special occasions such as holidays, vacations and birthdays. Since each LIFEPAC takes three to four weeks or 18 days to complete, it should take about 180 school days to finish a set of ten LIFEPACs. Starting at the beginning school date, mark off 18 school days on the calendar and that will become the targeted completion date for the first LIFEPAC. Continue marking the calendar until you have established dates for the remaining nine LIFEPACs making adjustments for previously noted holidays and vacations. If all five subjects are being used, the ten established target dates should be the same for the LIFEPACs in each subject.

# TEACHING SUPPLEMENTS

The sample weekly lesson plan and student grading sheet forms are included in this section as teacher support materials and may be duplicated at the convenience of the teacher.

The student grading sheet is provided for those who desire to follow the suggested guidelines for assignment of letter grades as previously discussed. The student's self test scores should be posted as percentage grades. When the LIFEPAC is completed the teacher should average the self test grades, multiply the average by .25 and post the points in the box marked self test points. The LIFEPAC percentage grade should be multiplied by .60 and posted. Next, the teacher should award and post points for written reports and oral work. A report may be any type of written work assigned to the student whether it is a LIFEPAC or additional learning activity. Oral work includes the student's ability to respond orally to questions which may or may not be related to LIFEPAC activities or any type of oral report assigned by the teacher. The points may then be totaled and a final grade entered along with the date that the LIFEPAC was completed.

The Student Record Book, which was specifically designed for use with the Alpha Omega curriculum, provides space to record weekly progress for one student over a nine-week period as well as a place to post self test and LIFEPAC scores. The Student Record Books are available through the current Alpha Omega catalog; however, unlike the enclosed forms these books are not for duplication and should be purchased in sets of four to cover a full academic year.

# WEEKLY LESSON PLANNER

Week of:

| | Subject | Subject | Subject | Subject |
|---|---|---|---|---|
| **Monday** | | | | |
| **Tuesday** | Subject | Subject | Subject | Subject |
| | | | | |
| **Wednesday** | Subject | Subject | Subject | Subject |
| | | | | |
| **Thursday** | Subject | Subject | Subject | Subject |
| | | | | |
| **Friday** | Subject | Subject | Subject | Subject |
| | | | | |

## WEEKLY LESSON PLANNER

Week of:

| | Subject | Subject | Subject | Subject |
|---|---|---|---|---|
| **Monday** | | | | |
| **Tuesday** | Subject | Subject | Subject | Subject |
| | | | | |
| **Wednesday** | Subject | Subject | Subject | Subject |
| | | | | |
| **Thursday** | Subject | Subject | Subject | Subject |
| | | | | |
| **Friday** | Subject | Subject | Subject | Subject |
| | | | | |

Student Name _____     Year _____

## Bible

| LP | Self Test Scores by Sections | | | | | Self Test Points | LIFEPAC Test | Oral Points | Report Points | Final Grade | Date |
|----|---|---|---|---|---|---|---|---|---|---|---|
|    | 1 | 2 | 3 | 4 | 5 | | | | | | |
| 01 | | | | | | | | | | | |
| 02 | | | | | | | | | | | |
| 03 | | | | | | | | | | | |
| 04 | | | | | | | | | | | |
| 05 | | | | | | | | | | | |
| 06 | | | | | | | | | | | |
| 07 | | | | | | | | | | | |
| 08 | | | | | | | | | | | |
| 09 | | | | | | | | | | | |
| 10 | | | | | | | | | | | |

## History & Geography

| LP | Self Test Scores by Sections | | | | | Self Test Points | LIFEPAC Test | Oral Points | Report Points | Final Grade | Date |
|----|---|---|---|---|---|---|---|---|---|---|---|
|    | 1 | 2 | 3 | 4 | 5 | | | | | | |
| 01 | | | | | | | | | | | |
| 02 | | | | | | | | | | | |
| 03 | | | | | | | | | | | |
| 04 | | | | | | | | | | | |
| 05 | | | | | | | | | | | |
| 06 | | | | | | | | | | | |
| 07 | | | | | | | | | | | |
| 08 | | | | | | | | | | | |
| 09 | | | | | | | | | | | |
| 10 | | | | | | | | | | | |

## Language Arts

| LP | Self Test Scores by Sections | | | | | Self Test Points | LIFEPAC Test | Oral Points | Report Points | Final Grade | Date |
|----|---|---|---|---|---|---|---|---|---|---|---|
|    | 1 | 2 | 3 | 4 | 5 | | | | | | |
| 01 | | | | | | | | | | | |
| 02 | | | | | | | | | | | |
| 03 | | | | | | | | | | | |
| 04 | | | | | | | | | | | |
| 05 | | | | | | | | | | | |
| 06 | | | | | | | | | | | |
| 07 | | | | | | | | | | | |
| 08 | | | | | | | | | | | |
| 09 | | | | | | | | | | | |
| 10 | | | | | | | | | | | |

Student Name _____     Year _____

## Math

| LP | Self Test Scores by Sections | | | | | Self Test Points | LIFEPAC Test | Oral Points | Report Points | Final Grade | Date |
|----|---|---|---|---|---|---|---|---|---|---|---|
| | 1 | 2 | 3 | 4 | 5 | | | | | | |
| 01 | | | | | | | | | | | |
| 02 | | | | | | | | | | | |
| 03 | | | | | | | | | | | |
| 04 | | | | | | | | | | | |
| 05 | | | | | | | | | | | |
| 06 | | | | | | | | | | | |
| 07 | | | | | | | | | | | |
| 08 | | | | | | | | | | | |
| 09 | | | | | | | | | | | |
| 10 | | | | | | | | | | | |

## Science

| LP | Self Test Scores by Sections | | | | | Self Test Points | LIFEPAC Test | Oral Points | Report Points | Final Grade | Date |
|----|---|---|---|---|---|---|---|---|---|---|---|
| | 1 | 2 | 3 | 4 | 5 | | | | | | |
| 01 | | | | | | | | | | | |
| 02 | | | | | | | | | | | |
| 03 | | | | | | | | | | | |
| 04 | | | | | | | | | | | |
| 05 | | | | | | | | | | | |
| 06 | | | | | | | | | | | |
| 07 | | | | | | | | | | | |
| 08 | | | | | | | | | | | |
| 09 | | | | | | | | | | | |
| 10 | | | | | | | | | | | |

## Spelling/Electives

| LP | Self Test Scores by Sections | | | | | Self Test Points | LIFEPAC Test | Oral Points | Report Points | Final Grade | Date |
|----|---|---|---|---|---|---|---|---|---|---|---|
| | 1 | 2 | 3 | 4 | 5 | | | | | | |
| 01 | | | | | | | | | | | |
| 02 | | | | | | | | | | | |
| 03 | | | | | | | | | | | |
| 04 | | | | | | | | | | | |
| 05 | | | | | | | | | | | |
| 06 | | | | | | | | | | | |
| 07 | | | | | | | | | | | |
| 08 | | | | | | | | | | | |
| 09 | | | | | | | | | | | |
| 10 | | | | | | | | | | | |

# INSTRUCTIONS FOR HISTORY & GEOGRAPHY

The LIFEPAC curriculum from grades 2 through 12 is structured so that the daily instructional material is written directly into the LIFEPACs. The student is encouraged to read and follow this instructional material in order to develop independent study habits. The teacher should introduce the LIFEPAC to the student, set a required completion schedule, complete teacher checks, be available for questions regarding both content and procedures, administer and grade tests, and develop additional learning activities as desired. Teachers working with several students may schedule their time so that students are assigned to a quiet work activity when it is necessary to spend instructional time with one particular student.

The third grade curriculum is an exploration of the history and geography of the United States. The intent of the course is to give the student an overview of the United States. The student will learn map terminology such as latitude, longitude, and compass rose. These terms and others will help the student discuss and understand the geography of the U.S. Geographical terms along with an overview of the geography of the U.S. will be introduced in the first LIFEPAC. The first LIFEPAC will also introduce the student to terms used in the study of resources and culture in later LIFEPACs.

Each LIFEPAC in 302-309 will introduce the student to a different region of the U.S. The curriculum will also introduce the student to the region's geography, climate, and resources. The student will also learn about key events in the history of the U.S. and the particular region. Famous individuals will also be highlighted in each LIFEPAC. The student will gain some general information about the founding of the U.S. He/she will also receive a general introduction to the U.S. government. Major industries of a region as well as places that people enjoy visiting will be introduced.

LIFEPAC 310 serves as a review of the U.S. regions. The student will receive one last overview of the geography of the U.S. He/she will also review the geography of those states east and west of the Mississippi River. Finally, the student will spend time reviewing each of the regions in the order in which they were taught. At the end of the course, the student should have a general understanding of the U.S.'s geography, history, and resources.

This course is not designed to be a comprehensive U.S. history or geography course. Instead it serves as an introduction to the geography of the U.S. as well as its history. The student will be introduced to each of the states but will not be given a comprehensive understanding of each. The student will gain an understanding of the characteristics of the various regions of the U.S. This will help the student to gain an overview of where each of the states is located as well as a general understanding of their characteristics.

This course is meant to stimulate a student's interest in the geography and history of the U.S. Ideally, the student will want to learn more about a particular region or state. This curriculum will serve as a foundation of a student's later study of geography in general and the U.S. in particular.

The Teacher Notes section of the Teacher's Guide lists the required or suggested materials for the LIFEPACs and provides additional learning activities for the students. The materials section refers only to LIFEPAC materials and does not include materials which may be needed for the additional activities. Additional learning activities provide a change from the daily school routine, encourage the student's interest in learning and may be used as a reward for good study habits.

# HISTORY & GEOGRAPHY 301

Unit 1: U.S. Geography & History Study Skills

# TEACHER NOTES

| MATERIALS NEEDED FOR LESSON | |
|---|---|
| Required | Suggested |
| • LIFEPAC<br>• paper<br>• pencils<br>• crayons | • dictionary<br>• atlas<br>• maps<br>• pictures or videos of the U.S. regions<br>• Internet or encyclopedias |

## INDEPENDENT STUDY ACTIVITY: YOUR STATE OR ANY STATE

As you study the various regions of the U.S., you and your student may find it interesting to study the state in which you live. If you do not live in a U.S. state, your student may choose a state that is of particular interest. In the study, the student will learn about the geography, history, resources, and people of the chosen state. The student should place all of their work in a folder. The student will need an encyclopedia or Internet access in order to complete the study. This activity can be repeated for any state that you find is particularly interesting. It could be a state in which friends or relatives live or a state to which travel is planned. Duplication masters are provided in Unit 301 of this book for the Your State activity and for the Any State activity.

## UNIT CROSSWORD PUZZLE REVIEW WORKSHEET:

A duplication master for a review activity is provided for this unit. After the student has completed the unit, have them complete it to prepare for the final LIFEPAC Test.

### » ANSWERS FOR THE REVIEW WORKSHEET

1. community
2. exports
3. legend
4. location
5. distorted
6. trade
7. rural
8. imports
9. urban
10. law

# ADDITIONAL LEARNING ACTIVITIES:

Choose those activities that best suit the needs and interests of your student.

### Section 1: Map Skills

1. Create flash cards for the vocabulary words the student will be learning. On one side of the flash card, the student should write the vocabulary word. On the other side, the student should draw a picture representing the vocabulary word. You may need to help the student decide on an appropriate picture to draw.

2. Give the student a map of the U.S. with longitude and latitude lines. Ask the student to find the approximate lines of latitude or longitude where he/she lives. Give the student latitude and longitude coordinates and ask the student to find the state in which the lines meet.

3. Find a game of Battleship and play it with your student. As you play the game, remind the student of how longitude and latitude coordinates are used.

### Section 2: Resources

1. Give the student a state or local map without a legend. Ask the student to create a legend for that map.

2. Ask the student to list three natural resources that can be found in their community. Ask the student to think of two human resources that they could provide.

3. Have the student keep track of all the goods and services they use in an hour. These services would include clothing, electricity, paper, and food. Encourage the student to recognize how interdependent people are on each other for their daily needs.

### Section 3: Community

1. Have the student create a list of five characteristics of being a good member of a church, school, family, or other community. If you teach a number of students, have them compare their lists. Note those items that appear on more than one list.

2. Ask the student to think of traditions that their family or community celebrates. Ask the student to discover how those traditions started and why they continue.

3. Invite the student to draw pictures of the many services they receive receives from the town or city community in which they live. Examples may include a library, police, firefighters, roads, and sidewalks.

### Explore the Internet:

The Internet can be a useful resource for additional activities and information. Visit the National Geographic Kids website for geographical games and other fun facts. Search the Internet for websites with interactive maps. Remember to monitor the sites your students visit.

### Administer the LIFEPAC Test.

# U.S. GEOGRAPHY AND HISTORY CROSSWORD PUZZLE REVIEW

community
distorted
exports
imports
law
legend
location
rural
trade
urban

## ACROSS

5. Misshapen
6. The buying and selling of goods
8. Items coming from other places
9. Area within a city
10. Rule for living

## DOWN

1. People living in a similar area
2. Items sold to others
3. Explanation on a map
4. A place
7. The area around the country

# » INDEPENDENT STUDY ACTIVITY: YOUR STATE

**Follow all directions carefully.**
**Check the box as you complete each activity.**

## GEOGRAPHY

Begin your study by learning about the geography of your home state.
For these activities you will need a good map of your state.
Ask your teacher to print a map of the outline of your state.
You will look up information on the geography of your state and place
it on the map.

☐　**Activity 1:** Find the names to three major rivers in your state.
　　Draw them on the map in blue. Label them in pencil.

☐　**Activity 2:** Find the names of three cities with the greatest population
　　in your state. If your state capital is not one of the three, add that as well.
　　Draw them on your map with red circles.
　　Use a red star to indicate your state's capital. Label the cities in pencil.

☐　**Activity 3:** Find the location of your home on the map.
　　Draw a circle in yellow where you live and label it as your home in pencil.

☐　**Activity 4:** Locate two major bodies of water, oceans, or lakes.
　　Draw them in purple and label them on your map.

☐　**Activity 5:** Locate any significant mountains or hills in your home state.
　　Draw them in  green and label them with pencil.

## EVENTS

Learn about important events in the settlement of your state.
Look at why these settlers came to your state and where they lived.

**Fill out the form with the following information. You may need to write the information on a separate sheet of paper so you have more room.**

The first explorers to my home state of _____ were

_____ .

More settlers followed because they wanted to  _____ .

Many settlers came from the country of _____ .

My state became a part of the U.S. in _____ .

An important event that occurred in my state was

_____

This event was important because

_____

## PEOPLE

**Fill out the form with the following information.**

One important person from my state was

_____

This person was important because  _____ .

A second important person from my state was

_____

This person was important because  _____ .

# RESOURCES

## Fill out the form with the following information.

An important natural resource in my state is _____ .

It is used to/for _____ .

A business that is important to my state is _____ .

It is important to my state because _____ .

It is located in _____ .


# PLACES

## Fill out the form with the following information.

An important place in my state is _____

_____ .

The reason it is important is because _____

_____ .

One place I would like to visit in my home state is _____

_____

because _____

_____

_____

_____ .

## » INDEPENDENT STUDY ACTIVITY: ANY STATE

**Follow all directions carefully.**
**Check the box as you complete each activity.**

# GEOGRAPHY

Begin your study by learning about the geography of any state you have chosen. For these activities you will need a good map of the state. Ask your teacher to print a map of the outline of the state. You will look up information on the geography of the state and place it on the map.

☐ **Activity 1:** Find the names to three major rivers in the state. Draw them on the map in blue. Label them in pencil.

☐ **Activity 2:** Find the names of three cities with the greatest population in the state. If the state capital is not one of the three, add that as well. Draw them on your map with red circles.
Use a red star to indicate the state's capital. Label the cities in pencil.

☐ **Activity 3:** Find the location of a city on the map that has special meaning. This could be a city where you used to live, where a friend or relative lives, or a city that you have heard about.
Draw a circle in yellow where this city is located and label it with the city name in pencil.

☐ **Activity 4:** Locate two major bodies of water, oceans, or lakes. Draw them in purple and label them on your map.

☐ **Activity 5:** Locate any significant mountains or hills in the state. Draw them in green and label them with pencil.

## EVENTS

Learn about important events in the settlement of this state.
Look at why these settlers came to the state and where they lived.

**Fill out the form with the following information. You may need to write the information on a separate sheet of paper so you have more room.**

The first explorers to the state of _____ were

_____ .

More settlers followed because they wanted to _____

_____ .

Many settlers came from the country of _____ .

This state became a part of the U.S. in _____ .

An important event that occurred in this state was _____

_____ .

This event was important because _____

_____ .

## PEOPLE

**Fill out the form with the following information.**

One important person from this state was _____

_____ .

This person was important because _____

_____ .

A second important person from this state was _____ .

This person was important because _____

_____ .

## RESOURCES

### Fill out the form with the following information.

An important natural resource in this state is _____ .

It is used to/for _____ .

A business that is important to this state is _____ .

It is important to the state because _____ .

It is located in _____ .


## PLACES

### Fill out the form with the following information.

An important place in this state is _____ .

The reason it is important is because _____ .

One place I would like to visit in this home state is _____

because _____

_____

_____ .

# ANSWER KEYS

## SECTION 1

| | |
|---|---|
| **1.1** | state boundary |
| **1.2** | state capital |
| **1.3** | north |
| **1.4** | river |
| **1.5** | Canada |
| **1.6** | Atlantic, Pacific |
| **1.7** | red circle, red star |
| **1.8** | California, Arizona, New Mexico, Texas |
| **1.9** | Minnesota |
| **1.10** | Bismark, Lansing, Richmond, Phoenix |
| **1.11** | Mississippi River |
| **1.12** | about 560 miles |
| **1.13** | about 280 miles |
| **1.14** | Teacher check |

## SELF TEST 1

| | |
|---|---|
| **1.01** | e |
| **1.02** | c |
| **1.03** | a |
| **1.04** | b |
| **1.05** | d |
| **1.06** | Arcadia |
| **1.07** | 12 |
| **1.08** | Any: Okeechobee, Glades, Hendry, Palm Beach, or Martin |
| **1.09** | Interstate 75 |
| **1.010** | about 130 miles |
| **1.011** | South |
| **1.012** | true |
| **1.013** | true |
| **1.014** | false |
| **1.015** | true |

# SECTION 2

**2.1**  basic needs
**2.2**  Renewable
**2.3**  non-renewable
**2.4**  Non-renewable
**2.5**  Renewable
**2.6**  false
**2.7**  true
**2.8**  true
**2.9**  Examples may include television, mattress, or pencil
**2.10**  Teacher check
**2.11**  Teacher check

# SELF TEST 2

**2.01**  N (non-renewable)
**2.02**  R (renewable)
**2.03**  R (renewable)
**2.04**  d
**2.05**  c
**2.06**  a
**2.07**  e
**2.08**  b
**2.09**  g
**2.010**  f
**2.011**  false
**2.012**  true
**2.013**  false
**2.014**  false
**2.015**  true
**2.016**  true

# SECTION 3

| | |
|---|---|
| **3.1** | citizen |
| **3.2** | rural |
| **3.3** | population |
| **3.4** | urban |
| **3.5** | community |
| **3.6** | false |
| **3.7** | true |
| **3.8** | false |
| **3.9** | false |
| **3.10** | true |
| **3.11** | Teacher check |
| **3.12** | Teacher check |

# SELF TEST 3

| | |
|---|---|
| **3.01** | e |
| **3.02** | f |
| **3.03** | a |
| **3.04** | c |
| **3.05** | b |
| **3.06** | d |
| **3.07** | true |
| **3.08** | false |
| **3.09** | false |
| **3.010** | true |
| **3.011** | false |
| **3.012** | true |
| **3.013** | a |
| **3.014** | c |
| **3.015** | a |
| **3.016** | b |
| **3.017** | c |

# LIFEPAC TEST

1.  d
2.  a
3.  f
4.  e
5.  c
6.  b
7.  b
8.  c
9.  b
10. c
11. a
12. c
13. true
14. false
15. true
16. false
17. true
18. true
19. true
20. Oregon
21. a red dot
22. Tulare
23. Interstate 5
24. Lake Tahoe
25. a black dashed line

# ALTERNATE LIFEPAC TEST

1.  c
2.  d
3.  e
4.  f
5.  a
6.  b
7.  b. consumer
8.  c. basic needs
9.  a. symbol
10. a. imports
11. b. computers
12. a. corn
13. c. equator
14. true
15. false
16. false
17. true
18. true
19. true
20. false
21. a black dot
22. about 22 miles
23. Madison
24. Illinois
25. Eau Claire

# HISTORY & GEOGRAPHY 301

## ALTERNATE LIFEPAC TEST

**NAME** _____

**DATE** _____

**SCORE** _____

**Each answer** = 1 point

## Draw a line to the correct answer.

**1.** urban ●

**2.** rural ●

**3.** citizen ●

**4.** population ●

**5.** cartographer ●

**6.** distorted ●

**a.** a map maker

**b.** misshapen

**c.** city

**d.** the area in the country

**e.** a member of a state or nation

**f.** the number of people who live in an area

**Write the correct answer on the blank.**

**7.** A person who buys goods is called a _____ .
   a. producer          b. consumer          c. buyer

**8.** Food, water, and shelter are considered _____ .
   a. non-renewable resources            b. services
   c. basic needs

**9.** A _____ is something which represents
   something else.
   a. symbol          b. legend          c. good

**10.** Items coming from other places are called _____ .
   a. imports          b. goods          c. exports

**11.** An example of a manufactured good is _____ .
   a. water          b. computers          c. coal

**12.** An example of a renewable resource is _____ .
   a. corn          b. coal          c. diamonds

**13.** The _____ is a famous line of latitude.
   a. north pole          b. border          c. equator

**Answer *true* or *false*.**

**14.** _____ A scale on a map helps you tell the distance
   between places.

**15.** _____ All maps show cities and towns.

**16.** _____ A car is an example of a basic need.

**17.** _____ In a diverse community, there are many different
   types of people.

**18.** _____ Each area of the United States has both natural
   and human resources.

**19.** _____ Laws help communities remain safe and peaceful.

**20.** _____ People can only be members of one community
   at a time.

## Answer the questions based on the map of Wisconsin.

**21.** What symbol is used to show a major town? _____

**22.** What is the distance from Racine to Milwaukee? _____

**23.** What is the capital city of Wisconsin? _____

**24.** What state borders Wisconsin to the south?

_____

**25.** Which city is farther north: Madison or Eau Claire?

_____

# HISTORY & GEOGRAPHY 302

Unit 2: New England States

# TEACHER NOTES

| MATERIALS NEEDED FOR LESSON | |
|---|---|
| Required | Suggested |
| • LIFEPAC<br>• paper<br>• pencils<br>• crayons | • dictionary<br>• atlas<br>• maps<br>• pictures or videos of the U.S. regions<br>• Internet or encyclopedias |

## INDEPENDENT STUDY ACTIVITY: YOUR STATE OR ANY STATE

As you study the various regions of the U.S., you and your student may find it interesting to study the state in which you live. If you do not live in a U.S. state, your student may choose a state that is of particular interest. In the study, the student will learn about the geography, history, resources, and people of the chosen state. The student should place all of their work in a folder. The student will need an encyclopedia or Internet access in order to complete the study. This activity can be repeated for any state that you find is particularly interesting. It could be a state in which friends or relatives live or a state to which travel is planned. Duplication masters are provided in Unit 301 of this book for the Your State activity and for the Any State activity.

## UNIT MATCHING WORKSHEET:

A duplication master for a review activity is provided for this unit. After the student has completed the unit, have them complete it to prepare for the final LIFEPAC Test.

### » ANSWERS FOR THE REVIEW WORKSHEET

1. Maine ➜ Toothpicks
2. Vermont ➜ Maple Syrup
3. Connecticut ➜ Insurance companies
4. Massachusetts ➜ Pilgrim Ship
5. New Hampshire ➜ Granite

# ADDITIONAL LEARNING ACTIVITIES

Choose those activities that best suit the needs and interests of your student.

### Section 1: New England Geography

1. Create flash cards for the vocabulary words the student will be learning. On one side of the flash card, the student should write the vocabulary word. On the other side, the student should draw a picture representing the vocabulary word. You may need to help the student decide on an appropriate picture to draw.

2. Give the student an empty map of the New England states. Have the student label the states, indicate the places and names of the capital cities, and add the significant land and water features.

3. Have the student discover the average January and July temperatures of each New England state. Have them use subtraction to determine the temperature differences.

4. Trace the voyage the Pilgrims took from England to New England.

### Section 2: New England Resources

1. With your student, find a recipe using maple syrup and make it together. You could also make pancakes with maple syrup on top.

2. Have the student choose one of the U.S. presidents that came from New England. Ask the student to write a paragraph about the president.

3. Ask the student to make a poster about the life cycle of a lobster.

### Section 3: New England Community

1. Discuss the Pilgrim's first Thanksgiving. Have the student create a list of five things for which he/she is thankful. Pray together using items from the list.

2. Compare and contrast what tools are available for students to learn in school today versus what students in the 1700s used. Consider computers, paper, books, pencils, and chalkboards.

3. New England is known for its beautiful fall foliage. Have students collect leaves and label the types of trees from which they came.

### Explore the Internet:

The Internet can be a useful resource for additional activities and information. Search these key words and phrases: Paul Revere, colonial clothing, colonial tools, colonial America, and Pilgrims. Remember to monitor the sites your students visit.

### Administer the LIFEPAC Test.

The test is to be administered in one session. Give no help except with directions.
Evaluate the tests and review areas where the students have done poorly.
Review the pages and activities that stress the concepts tested.
If necessary, administer the Alternate LIFEPAC Test.

# GEOGRAPHY AND HISTORY 302: NEW ENGLAND STATES REVIEW

Draw a line from the state to the correct item that represents that state.

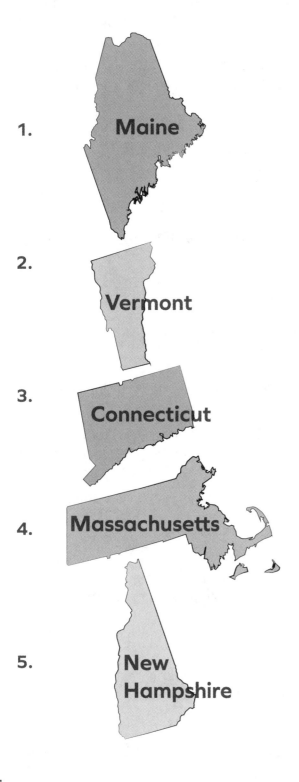

1.

2.

3.

4.

5.

# ANSWER KEYS

## SECTION 1

**1.1** Maine, New Hampshire, Vermont, Massachusetts, Connecticut, Rhode Island

**1.2** Augusta, Concord, Montpelier, Boston, Hartford, Providence

**1.3** Atlantic

**1.4** Massachusetts

**1.5** Vermont

**1.6** Augusta

**1.7** Green and White Mountains, Berkshires

**1.8** Maine

**1.9** Rhode Island

**1.10** Canada

**1.11** Connecticut

**1.12** Vermont

**1.13** Mount Washington

**1.14** Lake Champlain

**1.15** Nor'easter

**1.16** Gulf of Mexico

**1.17** ice (or snow)

## SELF TEST 1

**1.01** a

**1.02** c

**1.03** b

**1.04** b

**1.05** c

**1.06** true

**1.07** false

**1.08** false

**1.09** true

**1.010** false

**1.011** Maine

**1.012** Green

**1.013** Connecticut

**1.014** Champlain

**1.015** Gulf of Mexico

# SECTION 2

| | |
|---|---|
| **2.1** | e |
| **2.2** | d |
| **2.3** | a |
| **2.4** | c |
| **2.5** | b |
| **2.6** | John Adams |
| **2.7** | Paul Revere |
| **2.8** | Dr. Seuss |
| **2.9** | true |
| **2.10** | false |
| **2.11** | false |
| **2.12** | false |
| **2.13** | true |
| **2.14** | Teacher check |

# SELF TEST 2

| | |
|---|---|
| **2.01** | c |
| **2.02** | d |
| **2.03** | a |
| **2.04** | f |
| **2.05** | b |
| **2.06** | e |
| **2.07** | b |
| **2.08** | a |
| **2.09** | b |
| **2.010** | c |
| **2.011** | a |
| **2.012** | b |
| **2.013** | true |
| **2.014** | true |
| **2.015** | true |
| **2.016** | false |
| **2.017** | false |
| **2.018** | Teacher check |
| **2.019** | Teacher check |

# SECTION 3

**3.1** John Smith explored New England.
**3.2** Pilgrims settled in Massachusetts.
**3.3** A potato famine was in Ireland.
**3.4** Thousands of Irish immigrants came to New England.
**3.5** true
**3.6** false
**3.7** true
**3.8** false
**3.9** basketball
**3.10** leaves
**3.11** winter
**3.12** summer
**3.13** Teacher check

# SELF TEST 3

**3.01** c
**3.02** b
**3.03** b
**3.04** a
**3.05** a
**3.06** c
**3.07** b
**3.08** false
**3.09** false
**3.010** true
**3.011** true
**3.012** false
**3.013** true
**3.014** Teacher check

# LIFEPAC TEST

| | |
|---|---|
| **1.** | c |
| **2.** | b |
| **3.** | a |
| **4.** | c |
| **5.** | b |
| **6.** | a |
| **7.** | false |
| **8.** | true |
| **9.** | false |
| **10.** | false |
| **11.** | true |
| **12.** | true |
| **13.** | false |
| **14.** | false |
| **15.** | true |
| **16.** | buoy |
| **17.** | insurance |
| **18.** | Nor'easter |
| **19.** | Granite |
| **20.** | poet |
| **21.** | Maine |
| **22.** | Sap |
| **23.** | Rhode Island |
| **24.** | pot |
| **25.** | illustrator |

# ALTERNATE LIFEPAC TEST

| | |
|---|---|
| **1.** | true |
| **2.** | false |
| **3.** | true |
| **4.** | true |
| **5.** | false |
| **6.** | true |
| **7.** | true |
| **8.** | c |
| **9.** | e |
| **10.** | f |
| **11.** | a |
| **12.** | b |
| **13.** | d |
| **14.** | a. Maine |
| **15.** | c. Canada |
| **16.** | c. Berkshires |
| **17.** | b. Pilgrims |
| **18.** | a. Irish |
| **19.** | c. blueberries |
| **20.** | c. (both a. and b) come from Massachusetts *and* live in the White House |
| **21.** | a. Dr. Seuss |
| **22.** | c. Dr. Naismith |
| **23.** | c. average size |
| **24.** | b. stays above freezing |
| **25.** | b. leaves |

# HISTORY & GEOGRAPHY 302

ALTERNATE LIFEPAC TEST

NAME _____

DATE _____

SCORE _____

20
25

**Each answer** = 1 point

## Answer *true* or *false*.

1. _____ The first college founded in the United States was Harvard.

2. _____ Lake Champlain is on the border of Rhode Island and Massachusetts.

3. _____ Canada is located north of New England.

4. _____ The largest producer of toothpicks in the United States is Maine.

5. _____ People in New England enjoy skating and skiing during the summer.

6. _____ Vermont is the only New England state that does not touch the Atlantic Ocean.

7. _____ Paul Revere warned colonists that the British were coming.

## Draw a line to the correct answer.

8. illustrator ●

9. Nor'easter ●

10. pot ●

11. Maine ●

12. Massachusetts ●

13. immigrant ●

**a.** largest producer of toothpicks

**b.** location of the first U.S. college

**c.** a person who draws pictures for books

**d.** a person who moves to another country

**e.** a strong winter or fall storm

**f.** a cage used to catch lobster

## Write the correct answer on the blank.

14. _____ is the most northern New England state.
   a. Maine          b. Massachusetts     c. Connecticut

15. _____ is located to the north of New England.
   a. Mexico          b. England          c. Canada

16. The White Mountains, Green Mountains, and the _____ are located in New England.
   a. Purple Mountains     b. Rocky Mountains     c. Berkshires

17. The _____ came to New England because they wanted to worship God.
   a. Irish          b. Pilgrims          c. English

18. The _____ came to New England because of a potato famine.
   a. Irish          b. Pilgrims          c. English

19. The three largest producers of _____ are Maine, New Hampshire, and Massachusetts.
   a. potatoes          b. corn          c. blueberries

**20.** John Adams was the first U.S. president to _____

_____ .
a. come from Massachusetts
b. live in the White House
c. both a. and b.

**21.** _____ was a children's author and

illustrator.
a. Dr. Seuss           b. Emily Dickinson           c. Dr. Naismith

**22.** _____ was the inventor of

basketball.
a. Dr. Seuss           b. Emily Dickinson           c. Dr. Naismith

**23.** A lobster is kept if it is _____ .
a. small               b. pregnant                 c. average size

**24.** Maple trees are tapped when it _____ at night and

gets to 45 degrees during the day.
a. stays above freezing
b. freezes
c. snows

**25.** People come to New England in the fall to see the _____ .
a. skiers              b. leaves                   c. cranberries

# HISTORY & GEOGRAPHY 303

Unit 3: Mid-Atlantic States

# TEACHER NOTES

| MATERIALS NEEDED FOR LESSON | |
|---|---|
| Required | Suggested |
| • LIFEPAC<br>• paper<br>• pencils<br>• crayons | • dictionary<br>• atlas<br>• maps<br>• pictures or videos of the U.S. regions<br>• Internet or encyclopedias |

## INDEPENDENT STUDY ACTIVITY: YOUR STATE OR ANY STATE

As you study the various regions of the U.S., you and your student may find it interesting to study the state in which you live. If you do not live in a U.S. state, your student may choose a state that is of particular interest. In the study, the student will learn about the geography, history, resources, and people of the chosen state. The student should place all of their work in a folder. The student will need an encyclopedia or Internet access in order to complete the study. This activity can be repeated for any state that you find is particularly interesting. It could be a state in which friends or relatives live or a state to which travel is planned. Duplication masters are provided in Unit 301 of this book for the Your State activity and for the Any State activity.

## UNIT MATCHING WORKSHEET:

A duplication master for a review activity is provided for this unit. After the student has completed the unit, have them complete it to prepare for the final LIFEPAC Test.

### » ANSWERS FOR THE REVIEW WORKSHEET

| | |
|---|---|
| **3** | The Revolutionary War began. |
| **6** | The Civil War was fought. |
| **1** | The Pilgrims landed in Massachusetts. |
| **5** | The Revolutionary War ended. |
| **4** | The Declaration of Independence was written. |
| **2** | Harvard became the first university in the U.S. |

# ADDITIONAL LEARNING ACTIVITIES

Choose those activities that best suit the needs and interests of your student.

### Section 1: Mid-Atlantic Geography

1. Create flash cards for the vocabulary words the student will be learning. On one side of the flash card, the student should write the vocabulary word. On the other side, the student should draw a picture representing the vocabulary word. You may need to help the student decide on an appropriate picture to draw.

2. Choose one of the major cities in the Mid-Atlantic states. Help your student to graph the average monthly temperature of that city.

3. Ask the student to find the population of two major cities in the region. Have the student use subtraction to determine the population difference.

4. Have the student draw a map of the Chesapeake Bay. Locate five communities along the bay.

### Section 2: Mid-Atlantic Resources

1. Direct the student to draw a picture of a Washington D.C. landmark.

2. With the student, create a timeline of the U.S. presidents that came from the Mid-Atlantic region.

3. Discover three of Thomas Edison's inventions that led to devices people use today.

### Section 3: Mid-Atlantic Community

1. Create a chart of the three branches of government. List the parts and work of each branch.

2. Choose an important Supreme Court case and explain how the work of the court impacted the nation. Cases you might want to choose include Brown v. Board of Education (1954) and Dred Scott v. Sanford (1857).

3. Ask your student to imagine they were president of the U.S.
   What are three things the Student would like to promote or work on as president?

### Explore the Internet:

The Internet can be a useful resource for additional activities and information. Visit YouTube and search "I'm Just a Bill" from the television program *Schoolhouse Rock*. This segment describes how a bill becomes a law in musical terms. Search the Internet for the "PBS Kids Democracy Project" to learn more about the U.S. government. Use the key phrase "Lincoln Memorial" to find websites with information about this national monument. Remember to monitor the sites your students visit.

### Administer the LIFEPAC Test.

The test is to be administered in one session. Give no help except with directions. Evaluate the tests and review areas where the students have done poorly. Review the pages and activities that stress the concepts tested. If necessary, administer the Alternate LIFEPAC Test.

# GEOGRAPHY AND HISTORY 303: MID-ATLANTIC STATES REVIEW

**Put the following events from our nation's history in chronological order.**

☐ The Revolutionary War began.

☐ The Civil War was fought.

☐ The Pilgrims landed in Massachusetts.

☐ The Revolutionary War ended.

☐ The Declaration of Independence was written.

☐ Harvard became the first university in the U.S.

# ANSWER KEYS

## SECTION 1

**1.1** New York, Pennsylvania, New Jersey, Maryland, Delaware
**1.2** Washington, D.C.
**1.3** The Atlantic Ocean
**1.4** New Jersey and New York
**1.5** Albany, Harrisburg, Trenton, Annapolis, Dover
**1.6** The Chesapeake Bay
**1.7** The Appalachian Mountains
**1.8** The Hudson River
**1.9** Virginia, West Virginia
**1.10** Lake Erie, Lake Ontario
**1.11** b
**1.12** a
**1.13** c
**1.14** a
**1.15** a
**1.16** b
**1.17** true
**1.18** false
**1.19** true

## SELF TEST 1

**1.01** c
**1.02** a
**1.03** e
**1.04** d
**1.05** b
**1.06** true
**1.07** true
**1.08** false
**1.09** false
**1.010** false
**1.011** fertile
**1.012** rivers
**1.013** sandy
**1.014** largest
**1.015** highest

# SECTION 2

| | |
|---|---|
| **2.1** | false |
| **2.2** | true |
| **2.3** | false |
| **2.4** | false |
| **2.5** | true |
| **2.6** | four |
| **2.7** | two |
| **2.8** | 300 |
| **2.9** | France |
| **2.10** | Thomas Edison |
| **2.11** | b |
| **2.12** | c |
| **2.13** | c |
| **2.14** | b |
| **2.15** | Teacher check |

# SELF TEST 2

| | |
|---|---|
| **2.01** | c |
| **2.02** | e |
| **2.03** | d |
| **2.04** | a |
| **2.05** | b |
| **2.06** | b |
| **2.07** | c |
| **2.08** | c |
| **2.09** | b |
| **2.010** | c |
| **2.011** | a |
| **2.012** | a |
| **2.013** | false |
| **2.014** | true |
| **2.015** | true |
| **2.016** | false |
| **2.017** | true |
| **2.018** | false |
| **2.019** | Teacher check |
| **2.020** | Teacher check |

# SECTION 3

| | |
|---|---|
| **3.1** | Swedish |
| **3.2** | English |
| **3.3** | Maryland |
| **3.4** | Quakers |
| **3.5** | Ellis Island |
| **3.6** | true |
| **3.7** | false |
| **3.8** | false |
| **3.9** | false |
| **3.10** | true |
| **3.11** | Teacher check |
| **3.12** | three |
| **3.13** | Canada |
| **3.14** | New York City |
| **3.15** | Guggenheim |
| **3.16** | Washington, D.C. |
| **3.17** | two |
| **3.18** | Teacher check |

# SELF TEST 3

| | |
|---|---|
| **3.01** | c |
| **3.02** | e |
| **3.03** | a |
| **3.04** | b |
| **3.05** | d |
| **3.06** | b |
| **3.07** | a |
| **3.08** | a |
| **3.09** | c |
| **3.010** | c |
| **3.011** | c |
| **3.012** | true |
| **3.013** | true |
| **3.014** | false |
| **3.015** | true |
| **3.016** | false |
| **3.017** | true |
| **3.018** | false |
| **3.019** | Teacher check |
| **3.020** | Teacher check |

# LIFEPAC TEST

1. d
2. e
3. a
4. b
5. f
6. c
7. true
8. true
9. false
10. true
11. false
12. false
13. false
14. true
15. true
16. b
17. a
18. a
19. c
20. b
21. c
22. c
23. b
24. a
25. Teacher check

# ALTERNATE LIFEPAC TEST

1. true
2. false
3. true
4. true
5. false
6. true
7. true
8. b
9. e
10. a
11. c
12. d
13. New Jersey
14. Maryland
15. Delaware
16. New York
17. Washington, D.C.
18. Virginia
19. Pennsylvania
20. b. Philadelphia
21. a. Swedish
22. c. three
23. a. Executive
24. b. Ellis Island
25. c. Lake Placid
26. Teacher check

# HISTORY & GEOGRAPHY 303

## ALTERNATE LIFEPAC TEST

**NAME** _____

**DATE** _____

**SCORE** _____

**Each answer** = 1 point

## Answer *true* or *false.*

1. _____ The Piedmont Plateau has fertile soil.

2. _____ Niagara Falls is located on the border of New York and Pennsylvania.

3. _____ The Mid-Atlantic states have four seasons.

4. _____ The colony of Maryland welcomed Christians of all denominations.

5. _____ The Bill of Rights said that the United States was to be a democracy.

6. _____ As the U.S. government was formed, small states were worried the large states would have too much power.

7. _____ New York City is a cultural capital of the region and the United States.

## Draw a line to the correct answer.

8. Ben Franklin ●     **a.** was elected president four times

9. Thomas Jefferson ●     **b.** served as an ambassador to France during the Revolutionary War

10. Franklin Roosevelt ●

11. Harriet Tubman ●     **c.** led enslaved people to freedom

    **d.** invented the electric light bulb

12. Thomas Edison ●     **e.** wrote the Declaration of Independence

## Fill in the blank. Use the words from the word bank.

Delaware     Maryland     New Jersey
New York     Pennsylvania     Virginia
Washington, D.C.

13. _____ is known as the "Garden State."

14. Virginia and _____ surround the Chesapeake Bay.

15. Dover is the capital of _____ .

16. The Brooklyn Bridge connects Long Island and

_____ .

17. The Smithsonian Museum is located in

_____ .

18. West Virginia and _____ are located south of the Mid-Atlantic states.

19. The state of _____ is the only Mid-Atlantic state that does not touch the Atlantic Ocean.

## Write the correct answer on the blank.

**20.** The city of _____ served as a center of colonist activity during the Revolutionary War.

    a. Washington, D.C.    b. Philadelphia    c. Dover

**21.** Dutch and _____ settlers first lived in the New York area.

    a. Swedish    b. Irish    c. Italian

**22.** The United States has _____ branches of government.

    a. two    b. five    c. three

**23.** The president is the head of the _____ branch of government.

    a. Executive    b. Judicial    c. Legislative

**24.** _____ served as a center for immigrants arriving in the U.S. from the 1880s to 1950s.

    a. Long Island    b. Ellis Island    c. Rhode Island

**25.** Two Olympics were held at _____ .

    a. Niagara Falls    b. Lake Ontario    c. Lake Placid

## Short Answer.

**26.** What role has geography had in the types of jobs found in the Mid-Atlantic states?

_____

_____

_____

_____

# HISTORY & GEOGRAPHY 304

## Unit 4: Southern-Atlantic States

# TEACHER NOTES

| MATERIALS NEEDED FOR LESSON | |
| --- | --- |
| Required | Suggested |
| • LIFEPAC<br>• paper<br>• pencils<br>• crayons | • dictionary<br>• atlas<br>• maps<br>• pictures or videos of the U.S. regions<br>• Internet or encyclopedias |

## INDEPENDENT STUDY ACTIVITY: YOUR STATE OR ANY STATE

As you study the various regions of the U.S., you and your student may find it interesting to study the state in which you live. If you do not live in a U.S. state, your student may choose a state that is of particular interest. In the study, the student will learn about the geography, history, resources, and people of the chosen state. The student should place all of their work in a folder. The student will need an encyclopedia or Internet access in order to complete the study. This activity can be repeated for any state that you find is particularly interesting. It could be a state in which friends or relatives live or a state to which travel is planned. Duplication masters are provided in Unit 301 of this book for the Your State activity and for the Any State activity.

## UNIT MATCHING WORKSHEET:

A duplication master for a review activity is provided for this unit. After the student has completed the unit, have them complete it to prepare for the final LIFEPAC Test.

### » ANSWERS FOR THE REVIEW WORKSHEET

1. Jamestown
2. George Washington
3. Cape Canaveral
4. A
5. George Washington Carver

# ADDITIONAL LEARNING ACTIVITIES

Choose those activities that best suit the needs and interests of your student.

## Section 1: Southern-Atlantic Geography

1. Create flash cards for the vocabulary words the student will be learning. On one side of the flash card, the student should write the vocabulary word. On the other side, the student should draw a picture representing the vocabulary word. You may need to help the student decide on an appropriate picture to draw.

2. Help your student research how hurricanes are formed and tracked.

3. With your student explore the flora and fauna that can be found on the Outer Banks.

4. Eat citrus products like those from Florida with your student.

## Section 2: Southern-Atlantic Resources

1. Research one of the many presidents who came from the region.

2. Billy Graham's son, Franklin, has a ministry called Samaritan's Purse. One part of the ministry is entitled Operation Christmas Child where shoe boxes are filled with supplies and gifts for children living in poverty. Consider working with your student to participate in this or another service project to show God's love to others.

3. Listen to Martin Luther King, Jr.'s "I Have a Dream" speech.

## Section 3: Southern-Atlantic Community

1. Help your student research one of the first astronauts. Write a short report.

2. Go on a nature hike. Look at how the landscape of your area is similar or different from the landscape of the Southern Atlantic region.

3. Have your student create a poster to promote tourism in the Southern Atlantic region. Explain why people should come.

**Explore the Internet:**

The Internet can be a useful resource for additional activities and information. Search these key phrases: "Colonial Williamsburg" and "the Life of George Washington movie on Early America." Remember to monitor the sites your students visit.

**Administer the LIFEPAC Test.**

The test is to be administered in one session. Give no help except with directions. Evaluate the tests and review areas where the students have done poorly. Review the pages and activities that stress the concepts tested. If necessary, administer the Alternate LIFEPAC Test.

# HISTORY & GEOGRAPHY 304: SOUTHERN-ATLANTIC STATES REVIEW

**Fill in the blanks with the correct answers to review the first Southern-Atlantic states.**

1. The first permanent settlement in Virginia was _____ .

2. The first president of the U.S. was _____ .

3. The first astronaut was sent into space from _____ _____ , Florida.

4. The name of the first hurricane each year begins with the letter _____ .

5. The first person to develop over 300 peanut products was

    _____ .

# ANSWER KEYS

## SECTION 1

**1.1** West Virginia, Virginia, North Carolina, South Carolina, Georgia, Florida
**1.2** Charleston, Richmond, Raleigh, Columbia, Atlanta, Tallahassee
**1.3** East
**1.4** No
**1.5** North Carolina, Raleigh
**1.6** Florida
**1.7** Lake Okeechobee
**1.8** The Chattahoochee River
**1.9** Alabama
**1.10** Appalachian Mountains
**1.11** West Virginia
**1.12** d
**1.13** e
**1.14** b
**1.15** a
**1.16** f
**1.17** c
**1.18** true
**1.19** false
**1.20** true
**1.21** false

## SELF TEST 1

**1.01** c
**1.02** b
**1.03** b
**1.04** c
**1.05** a
**1.06** false
**1.07** true
**1.08** true
**1.09** true
**1.010** false
**1.011** 5
**1.012** Everglades
**1.013** West Virginia
**1.014** Gulf of Mexico
**1.015** West Virginia

## SECTION 2

| | |
|---|---|
| **2.1** | broiler |
| **2.2** | peanuts |
| **2.3** | North Carolina |
| **2.4** | tobacco |
| **2.5** | Shrimp |
| **2.6** | c |
| **2.7** | a |
| **2.8** | a |
| **2.9** | b |
| **2.10** | a |
| **2.11** | true |
| **2.12** | true |
| **2.13** | false |
| **2.14** | false |
| **2.15** | Teacher check |

## SELF TEST 2

| | |
|---|---|
| **2.01** | c |
| **2.02** | f |
| **2.03** | a |
| **2.04** | e |
| **2.05** | b |
| **2.06** | d |
| **2.07** | b |
| **2.08** | b |
| **2.09** | c |
| **2.010** | a |
| **2.011** | a |
| **2.012** | c |
| **2.013** | false |
| **2.014** | false |
| **2.015** | false |
| **2.016** | false |
| **2.017** | true |
| **2.018** | true |
| **2.019** | Teacher check |

# SECTION 3

| | |
|---|---|
| **3.1** | West Virginia |
| **3.2** | Ponce de Leon |
| **3.3** | James |
| **3.4** | African |
| **3.5** | false |
| **3.6** | false |
| **3.7** | true |
| **3.8** | true |
| **3.9** | false |
| **3.10** | true |
| **3.11** | true |
| **3.12** | false |
| **3.13** | Teacher check |

# SELF TEST 3

| | |
|---|---|
| **3.01** | b |
| **3.02** | a |
| **3.03** | a |
| **3.04** | c |
| **3.05** | b |
| **3.06** | a |
| **3.07** | b |
| **3.08** | true |
| **3.09** | true |
| **3.010** | false |
| **3.011** | true |
| **3.012** | true |
| **3.013** | false |
| **3.014** | false |
| **3.015** | false |
| **3.016** | Example answers: |

– Some early settlers were looking for gold.
– Ponce de Leon explored Florida looking for gold and the fountain of youth.
– Space exploration takes place at Cape Canaveral and the Kennedy Space Center.

## LIFEPAC TEST

1. b
2. c
3. a
4. a
5. b
6. a
7. true
8. false
9. false
10. true
11. false
12. false
13. true
14. true
15. false
16. George Washington
17. Virginia
18. Outer Banks
19. West Virginia
20. broilers
21. John Smith
22. Florida
23. Ponce de Leon
24. West Virginia
25. astronaut

## ALTERNATE LIFEPAC TEST

1. false
2. true
3. true
4. true
5. false
6. false
7. true
8. b
9. e
10. d
11. c
12. f
13. a
14. b. Everglades
15. c. West Virginia
16. a. Mount Vernon
17. b. Civil
18. c. citrus crops
19. a. Atlanta
20. b. true
21. c. Jamestown
22. c. John F. Kennedy
23. b. the Fountain of Youth
24. a. 1969
25. c. Florida

# HISTORY & GEOGRAPHY 304

## ALTERNATE LIFEPAC TEST

NAME _____

DATE _____

SCORE _____

**Each answer** = 1 point

## Answer *true* or *false*.

1. _____ The Outer Banks are located off the coast of Florida.

2. _____ West Virginia is the only state in this region not located along the Atlantic coast.

3. _____ Hurricanes are named after men and women.

4. _____ Tobacco and sweet potatoes are grown in the Piedmont Plateau area.

5. _____ The Jamestown Colony was settled by the Spanish.

6. _____ Africans willingly came to the U.S. to work on plantations.

7. _____ The Blue Ridge Parkway is located in the Appalachian Mountains.

## Draw a line to the correct answer.

8.  George Washington          ●          **a.** explored Florida

9.  George Washington Carver ●          **b.** first president of the U.S.

10. Billy Graham                ●          **c.** led the Jamestown Colony

11. John Smith                  ●          **d.** preached at crusades

12. Martin Luther King, Jr.     ●          **e.** used peanuts to make many
                                                products
13. Ponce de Leon               ●          **f.** leader in the Civil Rights
                                                movement

## Write the correct answer on the blank.

14. The _____ is home to alligators,
    snakes, and birds.
    a.  Piedmont Plateau    b.  Everglades          c.  Outer Banks

15. The worst coal-mining disaster in the U.S. was in the state of
    _____ .
    a.  Georgia             b.  Virginia             c.  West Virginia

16. George Washington's home was named _____ .
    a.  Mount Vernon        b.  Cape Washington   c.  Grand Villa

17. The state of West Virginia was formed during the
    _____ War.
    a.  Revolutionary       b.  Civil                c.  French and Indian

18. Freezing weather in Florida damages _____ .
    a.  beaches             b.  the Everglades       c.  citrus crops

19. The home of Coca-Cola and CNN news is _____ .
    a.  Atlanta             b.  Columbia             c.  Raleigh

20. The word "infallible" means _____ .
    a.  wonderful           b.  true                 c.  dangerous

21. The _____ community ended
    because of disease, famine, and Native American attacks.
    a. Williamsburg          b. Mount Vernon          c. Jamestown

22. The Space Center at Cape Canaveral is named after
    _____ .
    a. George Washington
    b. Abraham Lincoln
    c. John F. Kennedy

23. Ponce de Leon searched for gold and _____
    _____ .
    a. the Lost City
    b. the Fountain of Youth
    c. the Endless Light

24. In _____ the first people traveled safely to the Moon and
    back.
    a. 1969                 b. 2002                 c. 1922

25. Disney World, Sea World, and many other parks and resorts are
    located in _____ .
    a. Virginia             b. South Carolina       c. Florida

# HISTORY & GEOGRAPHY 305

## Unit 5: Southern States

# TEACHER NOTES

| MATERIALS NEEDED FOR LESSON | |
|---|---|
| Required | Suggested |
| • LIFEPAC<br>• paper<br>• pencils<br>• crayons | • dictionary<br>• atlas<br>• maps<br>• pictures or videos of the U.S. regions<br>• Internet or encyclopedias |

## INDEPENDENT STUDY ACTIVITY: YOUR STATE OR ANY STATE

As you study the various regions of the U.S., you and your student may find it interesting to study the state in which you live. If you do not live in a U.S. state, your student may choose a state that is of particular interest. In the study, the student will learn about the geography, history, resources, and people of the chosen state. The student should place all of their work in a folder. The student will need an encyclopedia or Internet access in order to complete the study. This activity can be repeated for any state that you find is particularly interesting. It could be a state in which friends or relatives live or a state to which travel is planned. Duplication masters are provided in Unit 301 of this book for the Your State activity and for the Any State activity.

## UNIT MATCHING WORKSHEET:

A duplication master for a review activity is provided for this unit. After the student has completed the unit, have them complete it to prepare for the final LIFEPAC Test.

### » ANSWERS FOR THE REVIEW WORKSHEET

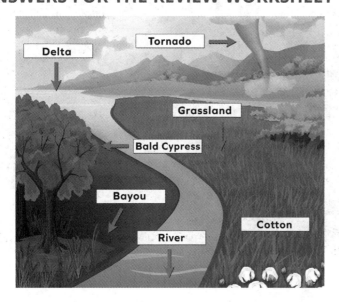

# ADDITIONAL LEARNING ACTIVITIES

Choose those activities that best suit the needs and interests of your student.

### Section 1: Southern Geography

1. Create flash cards for the vocabulary words the student will be learning. On one side of the flash card, the student should write the vocabulary word. On the other side, the student should draw a picture representing the vocabulary word. You may need to help the student decide on an appropriate picture to draw.

2. Help your student study some of the environmental issues affecting the Gulf Coast region.

3. Have the student research some of the plants and animals that live in the Louisiana bayous.

4. Ask the student to find the names of the longest rivers on each continent. Ask the student to compare their lengths with the Mississippi and Missouri Rivers.

### Section 2: Southern Resources

1. Discover some of the products that can be made from cotton.

2. Have the student write a sentence using the Braille system.

3. Locate places around the country that were named for Daniel Boone.

### Section 3: Southern Community

1. Have the student write an imaginary letter to a famous person from the region. What would you like to ask them?

2. Have the student create a diorama of a Southern plantation home.

3. Ask the student to research the history of the Creole people who live in the Southern states.

### Explore the Internet:

The Internet can be a useful resource for additional activities and information.
Search "Native Americans of the Southeast" to learn more about Native Americans in this region. Perhaps research a specific native group, such as Creek, Seminole, Cherokee, or Choctaw. Visit the U.S. Mint's website for a variety of information as well as interactive games for kids. Remember to monitor the sites your students visit.

### Administer the LIFEPAC Test.

The test is to be administered in one session. Give no help except with directions.
Evaluate the tests and review areas where the students have done poorly.
Review the pages and activities that stress the concepts tested.
If necessary, administer the Alternate LIFEPAC Test.

# HISTORY & GEOGRAPHY 305: SOUTHERN STATES REVIEW

Identify the geographical features using words from the word bank.

| Bald Cypress | Bayou | Cotton | Delta |
| Grassland | River | Tornado | |

# ANSWER KEYS

## SECTION 1

**1.1**  Texas, Louisiana, Mississippi, Alabama
**1.2**  Kentucky, Tennessee, Arkansas, Mississippi, Louisiana
**1.3**  Montgomery, Little Rock, Frankfort, Baton Rouge, Jackson, Oklahoma City, Nashville, Austin
**1.4**  Kentucky
**1.5**  Texas
**1.6**  Tennessee
**1.7**  Texas, Oklahoma
**1.8**  Texas, Louisiana
**1.9**  Mexico
**1.10**  Texas
**1.11**  Mississippi
**1.12**  delta
**1.13**  bald cypress
**1.14**  bayou
**1.15**  false
**1.16**  false
**1.17**  true
**1.18**  true

## SELF TEST 1

**1.01**  d
**1.02**  e
**1.03**  a
**1.04**  c
**1.05**  b
**1.06**  true
**1.07**  false
**1.08**  false
**1.09**  true
**1.010**  true
**1.011**  Gulf of Mexico
**1.012**  Texas
**1.013**  tornado
**1.014**  Antarctica
**1.015**  Kentucky

## SECTION 2

| | |
|---|---|
| **2.1** | false |
| **2.2** | false |
| **2.3** | true |
| **2.4** | false |
| **2.5** | true |
| **2.6** | Oklahoma |
| **2.7** | Wilderness Road |
| **2.8** | Trail of Tears |
| **2.9** | Helen Keller |
| **2.10** | Kentucky |
| **2.11** | true |
| **2.12** | false |
| **2.13** | false |
| **2.14** | true |
| **2.15** | false |

## SELF TEST 2

| | |
|---|---|
| **2.01** | c |
| **2.02** | e |
| **2.03** | a |
| **2.04** | b |
| **2.05** | d |
| **2.06** | b |
| **2.07** | a |
| **2.08** | a |
| **2.09** | c |
| **2.010** | c |
| **2.011** | b |
| **2.012** | c |
| **2.013** | false |
| **2.014** | false |
| **2.015** | true |
| **2.016** | true |
| **2.017** | false |

# SECTION 3

| | |
|---|---|
| **3.1** | e |
| **3.2** | d |
| **3.3** | c |
| **3.4** | a |
| **3.5** | b |
| **3.6** | Teacher check |
| **3.7** | false |
| **3.8** | false |
| **3.9** | true |
| **3.10** | false |
| **3.11** | Kentucky Derby |
| **3.12** | Ash Wednesday |
| **3.13** | Bath houses |
| **3.14** | Teacher check |

# SELF TEST 3

| | |
|---|---|
| **3.01** | a |
| **3.02** | c |
| **3.03** | b |
| **3.04** | b |
| **3.05** | c |
| **3.06** | b |
| **3.07** | a |
| **3.08** | true |
| **3.09** | false |
| **3.010** | false |
| **3.011** | true |
| **3.012** | false |
| **3.013** | false |
| **3.014** | b |
| **3.015** | e |
| **3.016** | a |
| **3.017** | c |
| **3.018** | d |

## LIFEPAC TEST

1. b
2. a
3. b
4. c
5. b
6. c
7. false
8. true
9. true
10. false
11. true
12. true
13. true
14. false
15. true
16. country
17. Elvis Presley
18. Spain
19. Cotton
20. dude
21. Walmart
22. horse
23. Oklahoma
24. Daniel Boone
25. Mexico

## ALTERNATE LIFEPAC TEST

1. true
2. true
3. false
4. true
5. false
6. true
7. true
8. d
9. f
10. a
11. e
12. c
13. b
14. jazz
15. country
16. Kentucky
17. Sam Houston
18. president
19. Alamo
20. Helen Keller
21. Daniel Boone
22. Elvis Presley
23. Mexico
24. cotton
25. Tennessee

# HISTORY & GEOGRAPHY 305

## ALTERNATE LIFEPAC TEST

NAME _____

DATE _____

SCORE _____

**Each answer** = 1 point

## Answer *true* or *false*.

1. _____ Cotton seed oil is found in margarine and mayonnaise.

2. _____ Antarctica is the only continent that does not get tornadoes.

3. _____ The Mississippi River is the longest river in the U.S.

4. _____ Blues music had its beginnings in slave songs.

5. _____ A dude ranch is a ranch that only has horses.

6. _____ The Trail of Tears was the journey the Native Americans took when they were forced from their homes in the eastern U.S.

7. _____ Multiple wells can be drilled from one oil rig.

## Draw a line to the correct answer.

8. delta ●
9. bayou ●
10. abolished ●
11. seceded ●
12. crude oil ●
13. Braille ●

**a.** ended; stopped
**b.** a way of writing for the blind
**c.** oil taken directly from the ground
**d.** located at the mouth of a river
**e.** left; removed
**f.** a slow moving river in a flat area

## Fill in the blank.

14. The home of _____ music is New Orleans.
15. The home of _____ music is Nashville.
16. The _____ Derby is a famous horse race held each year.
17. _____ served as a president, senator, and governor in Texas.
18. Jefferson Davis was _____ of the Confederate States during the Civil War.
19. "Remember the _____ !" became a famous cry during the war between Texas and Mexico.
20. Even though she was deaf and blind, _____ traveled to many countries.
21. _____ helped build the Wilderness Road.
22. _____ was a famous rock 'n roll musician.

23. The country of _____ is south of Texas.

24. Before the Civil War, enslaved people were forced to do the hard work of picking _____ .

25. The Cumberland Gap is located at the crossroads of Kentucky, Virginia, and _____ .

# HISTORY & GEOGRAPHY 306

## Unit 6: Great Lakes States

# TEACHER NOTES

| MATERIALS NEEDED FOR LESSON | |
|---|---|
| Required | Suggested |
| • LIFEPAC<br>• paper<br>• pencils<br>• crayons | • dictionary<br>• atlas<br>• maps<br>• pictures or videos of the U.S. regions<br>• Internet or encyclopedias |

## INDEPENDENT STUDY ACTIVITY: YOUR STATE OR ANY STATE

As you study the various regions of the U.S., you and your student may find it interesting to study the state in which you live. If you do not live in a U.S. state, your student may choose a state that is of particular interest. In the study, the student will learn about the geography, history, resources, and people of the chosen state. The student should place all of their work in a folder. The student will need an encyclopedia or Internet access in order to complete the study. This activity can be repeated for any state that you find is particularly interesting. It could be a state in which friends or relatives live or a state to which travel is planned. Duplication masters are provided in Unit 301 of this book for the Your State activity and for the Any State activity.

## UNIT REVIEW WORKSHEET:

A duplication master for a review activity is provided for this unit. After the student has completed the unit, have them complete it to prepare for the final LIFEPAC Test.

### » ANSWERS FOR THE REVIEW WORKSHEET

# ADDITIONAL LEARNING ACTIVITIES

Choose those activities that best suit the needs and interests of your student.

## Section 1: Great Lakes Geography

1. Create flash cards for the vocabulary words the student will be learning. On one side of the flash card, the student should write the vocabulary word. On the other side, the student should draw a picture representing the vocabulary word. You may need to help the student decide on an appropriate picture to draw.

2. With your student, research some of the invasive species that are or have threatened the Great Lakes. Discover how these species came into the lakes and what is being done to prevent others from entering.

3. Give the student a map. Ask the student to find the average snow fall of five cities along the Great Lakes. Make sure some of the cities are located on the western coasts and others on the eastern coasts so students can see the impact of lake effect.

4. Study snowflakes with the student. Look at the differences among the many snowflakes that fall.

## Section 2: Great Lakes Resources

1. Create a timeline of the history of the automobile.

2. Have the student write an article for a newspaper as if they had watched the first flight of the Wright brothers.

3. Make popcorn and enjoy it with your student as you celebrate one of the crops from the Great Lakes states.

## Section 3: Great Lakes Community

1. Have the student create a flag for the Great Lakes region. The student should explain the design of the flag they created.

2. Help the student create an acrostic to review the Great Lakes states. Use the word "Great Lakes" for the acrostic. Have each letter stand for something the student learned about the region.

3. Help the student research a regional artist. Describe how their art captured the scenery or people of the region.

### Explore the Internet:

The Internet can be a useful resource for additional activities and information.
Search these key phrases: Orville and Wilbur Wright, Wright brothers, and Model T.
Remember to monitor the sites your students visit

### Administer the LIFEPAC Test.

The test is to be administered in one session. Give no help except with directions.
Evaluate the tests and review areas where the students have done poorly.
Review the pages and activities that stress the concepts tested.
If necessary, administer the Alternate LIFEPAC Test.

# HISTORY & GEOGRAPHY 306: GREAT LAKES STATES REVIEW

Write in the names of the Great Lakes states.
Can you name the lakes too?

# ANSWER KEYS

## SECTION 1

**1.1**  a.  Lake Huron
 b.  Lake Ontario
 c.  Lake Michigan
 d.  Lake Erie
 `e.  Lake Superior
**1.2**  Lake Michigan
**1.3**  Lake Superior
**1.4**  Lakes Superior, Michigan, Huron, and Erie
**1.5**  a.  St. Paul
 b.  Madison
 c.  Lansing
 d.  Springfield
 e.  Indianapolis
 f.  Columbus
**1.6**  Canada
**1.7**  Minnesota, Wisconsin, and Illinois
**1.8**  Minnesota
**1.9**  Ohio
**1.10**  Illinois
**1.11**  Wisconsin, Illinois, Indiana, and Michigan
**1.12**  Minnesota
**1.13**  Ohio River
**1.14**  Michigan
**1.15**  Lake Superior
**1.16**  Alaska
**1.17**  false
**1.18**  false
**1.19**  true

## SELF TEST 1

**1.01**  b
**1.02**  a
**1.03**  b
**1.04**  b
**1.05**  c
**1.06**  false
**1.07**  false
**1.08**  true
**1.09**  true
**1.010**  true
**1.011**  Ohio
**1.012**  Minnesota
**1.013**  snow
**1.014**  tributary
**1.015**  Wisconsin

## SECTION 2

| | |
|---|---|
| **2.1** | c |
| **2.2** | d |
| **2.3** | e |
| **2.4** | b |
| **2.5** | a |
| **2.6** | Ohio |
| **2.7** | Civil |
| **2.8** | assassinated |
| **2.9** | Rochester, Minnesota |
| **2.10** | surgery |
| **2.11** | Teacher check |
| **2.12** | true |
| **2.13** | false |
| **2.14** | false |
| **2.15** | true |
| **2.16** | true |

## SELF TEST 2

| | |
|---|---|
| **2.01** | c |
| **2.02** | a |
| **2.03** | e |
| **2.04** | f |
| **2.05** | d |
| **2.06** | b |
| **2.07** | b |
| **2.08** | a |
| **2.09** | b |
| **2.010** | c |
| **2.011** | a |
| **2.012** | b |
| **2.013** | false |
| **2.014** | false |
| **2.015** | true |
| **2.016** | true |
| **2.017** | true |

# SECTION 3

| | |
|---|---|
| **3.1** | missionaries |
| **3.2** | Michigan |
| **3.3** | Canada |
| **3.4** | Paris |
| **3.5** | false |
| **3.6** | true |
| **3.7** | true |
| **3.8** | false |
| **3.9** | Chicago |
| **3.10** | Willis |
| **3.11** | ice |
| **3.12** | Michigan |
| **3.13** | Teacher check |

# SELF TEST 3

| | |
|---|---|
| **3.01** | e |
| **3.02** | d |
| **3.03** | a |
| **3.04** | b |
| **3.05** | c |
| **3.06** | b |
| **3.07** | c |
| **3.08** | a |
| **3.09** | b |
| **3.010** | c |
| **3.011** | c |
| **3.012** | true |
| **3.013** | false |
| **3.014** | true |
| **3.015** | false |
| **3.016** | true |
| **3.017** | true |

## LIFEPAC TEST

1. c
2. a
3. c
4. c
5. a
6. c
7. true
8. true
9. false
10. false
11. true
12. true
13. false
14. true
15. false
16. Superior
17. Michigan
18. Minnesota
19. airplane
20. Moon
21. hospital
22. Abraham Lincoln
23. French
24. Paris
25. 500

## ALTERNATE LIFEPAC TEST

1. false
2. true
3. false
4. false
5. true
6. false
7. false
8. c
9. f
10. a
11. e
12. b
13. d
14. Illinois
15. Huron
16. east
17. zipper
18. Chicago
19. Henry Ford
20. fish
21. log cabin
22. Civil
23. France
24. Mississippi
25. French

# HISTORY & GEOGRAPHY 306

ALTERNATE LIFEPAC TEST

NAME _____

DATE _____

SCORE _____

**Each answer** = 1 point

## Answer *true* or *false*.

1. _____ Lake Superior is the only one of the Great Lakes entirely in the U.S.

2. _____ Lake Erie is the only one of the Great Lakes that regularly freezes over in the winter.

3. _____ Lake Michigan is the largest freshwater lake in the world.

4. _____ Henry Ford invented masking tape.

5. _____ Orville and Wilbur Wright were the first people to successfully build and fly an airplane.

6. _____ Abraham Lincoln was assassinated before the end of the Civil War.

7. _____ The Spanish explored the Great Lakes region.

## Draw a line to the correct answer.

8. tributary   •
9. patent   •
10. pasteurize   •
11. curd   •
12. dedication   •
13. invasive species   •

a. to heat milk to a high temperature to kill bacteria

b. a ceremony to devote a place for a purpose

c. a river which flows into another river or body of water

d. plants or animals that are not naturally found in a region

e. the solid substance that is separated from whey

f. a document which gives inventors certain rights

## Fill in the blank.

14. The Ohio River serves as the southern border of the states of Ohio, Indiana, and _____ .

15. The five Great Lakes are Lakes Erie, Ontario, _____ , Michigan, and Superior.

16. Lake effect snow generally falls to the south and _____ of the Great Lakes.

17. Until Whitcomb Judson invented the _____ most pants and coats were tied with buttons.

18. The tallest building in the U.S. is the Willis Tower located in the city of _____ .

19. _____ was able to mass produce cars with the assembly line.

20. Some people build ice houses so they can be comfortable while they _____ during the winter.

**21.** Abraham Lincoln was born in a _____ .

**22.** Lincoln was president during the _____ War.

**23.** Jacques Cartier claimed what is now Canada for

_____ .

**24.** Marquette and Joliet traveled down the

_____ River as far as Arkansas.

**25.** The Native Americans sided with the _____

during the war between the British and French.

# HISTORY & GEOGRAPHY 307

## Unit 7: Midwestern States

# TEACHER NOTES

| MATERIALS NEEDED FOR LESSON | |
|---|---|
| Required | Suggested |
| • LIFEPAC<br>• paper<br>• pencils<br>• crayons | • dictionary<br>• atlas<br>• maps<br>• pictures or videos of the U.S. regions<br>• Internet or encyclopedias |

## INDEPENDENT STUDY ACTIVITY: YOUR STATE OR ANY STATE

As you study the various regions of the U.S., you and your student may find it interesting to study the state in which you live. If you do not live in a U.S. state, your student may choose a state that is of particular interest. In the study, the student will learn about the geography, history, resources, and people of the chosen state. The student should place all of their work in a folder. The student will need an encyclopedia or Internet access in order to complete the study. This activity can be repeated for any state that you find is particularly interesting. It could be a state in which friends or relatives live or a state to which travel is planned. Duplication masters are provided in Unit 301 of this book for the Your State activity and for the Any State activity.

## UNIT REVIEW WORKSHEET:

A duplication master for a review activity is provided for this unit. After the student has completed the unit, have them complete it to prepare for the final LIFEPAC Test.

## » ANSWERS FOR THE REVIEW WORKSHEET

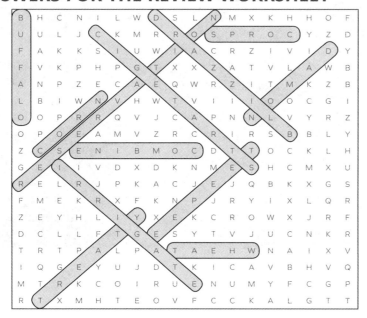

# ADDITIONAL LEARNING ACTIVITIES

Choose those activities that best suit the needs and interests of your student.

## Section 1: Midwestern Geography

1. Create flash cards for the vocabulary words the student will be learning. On one side of the flash card, the student should write the vocabulary word. On the other side, the student should draw a picture representing the vocabulary word. You may need to help the student decide on an appropriate picture to draw.

2. Have the student make a poster of the life cycle of a tornado.

3. Have the student alphabetize information such as state capitals and state names.

4. Sing "This is My Father's World." Discuss how people are to care for their Father's world.

## Section 2: Midwestern Resources

1. Read Little House on the Prairie by Laura Ingalls Wilder with your student.

2. Use kernels of corn in math exercises. Have students put the kernels in different subsets or use them in multiplication or division.

3. The early settlers needed to make their own butter. Find some instructions and make butter with your student.

## Section 3: Midwestern Community

1. Play games with your student that pioneer children played. Games include checkers, hopscotch, tic-tac-toe, three-legged races, jacks, and tag.

2. Make bread with the student.

3. Help the student create an art piece with seeds of food grown in the Midwest such as corn, beans, and other seeds.

### Explore the Internet:

The Internet can be a useful resource for additional activities and information.
Search "Lewis and Clark" to learn more about the Corps of Discovery. Visit the National Geographic website to play an interactive game about the Lewis and Clark Expedition.
Remember to monitor the sites your students visit.

### Administer the LIFEPAC Test.

The test is to be administered in one session. Give no help except with directions.
Evaluate the tests and review areas where the students have done poorly.
Review the pages and activities that stress the concepts tested.
If necessary, administer the Alternate LIFEPAC Test.

# HISTORY & GEOGRAPHY 307: MIDWEST STATES WORD SEARCH

| B | H | C | N | I | L | W | D | S | L | N | M | X | K | H | H | O | F |
| U | U | L | J | C | K | M | R | R | O | S | P | R | O | C | Y | Z | D |
| F | A | K | K | S | I | U | W | I | A | C | R | Z | I | V | I | D | Y |
| F | V | K | P | H | P | G | T | X | X | Z | A | T | V | L | A | W | B |
| A | N | P | Z | E | C | A | E | Q | W | R | Z | I | T | M | K | Z | B |
| L | B | I | W | N | V | H | W | T | V | I | I | I | O | O | C | G | I |
| O | O | P | R | R | Q | V | J | C | A | P | N | N | L | V | Y | R | Z |
| O | P | O | E | A | M | V | Z | R | C | R | I | R | S | B | B | L | Y |
| Z | C | S | E | N | I | B | M | O | C | D | T | T | O | C | K | L | H |
| G | E | I | I | V | D | X | D | K | N | M | E | S | H | C | M | X | U |
| R | E | L | R | J | P | K | A | C | J | E | J | Q | B | K | X | G | S |
| F | M | E | K | R | X | F | K | N | P | J | R | Y | I | X | L | Q | R |
| Z | E | Y | H | L | I | Y | X | E | K | C | R | O | W | X | J | R | F |
| D | C | L | L | F | T | G | E | S | Y | T | V | J | U | C | N | K | R |
| T | R | T | P | A | L | P | A | T | A | E | H | W | N | A | I | X | V |
| I | Q | G | E | Y | U | J | D | T | K | I | C | A | V | B | H | V | Q |
| M | T | R | K | C | O | I | R | U | E | N | U | M | Y | F | C | G | P |
| R | T | X | M | H | T | E | O | V | F | C | C | K | A | L | G | T | T |

| | | | |
|---|---|---|---|
| blizzard | buffalo | combine | corn |
| corps | irrigate | nomad | reservation |
| strategic | teepee | treaty | wheat |

# ANSWER KEYS

## SECTION 1

**1.1**  a.  Bismarck
      b.  Pierre
      c.  Lincoln
      d.  Topeka
      e.  Des Moines
      f.  Jefferson City
**1.2**  North Dakota, South Dakota, Nebraska, Kansas, Iowa, and Missouri
**1.3**  Iowa and Missouri
**1.4**  North Dakota, South Dakota, Nebraska, Kansas
**1.5**  Missouri
**1.6**  Nebraska and Kansas
**1.7**  Canada
**1.8**  Missouri
**1.9**  Iowa
**1.10**  Bismarck, North Dakota
**1.11**  longest
**1.12**  Montana
**1.13**  Black Hills
**1.14**  Ozarks
**1.15**  false
**1.16**  true
**1.17**  true
**1.18**  true
**1.19**  false

## SELF TEST 1

**1.01**  a
**1.02**  c
**1.03**  b
**1.04**  a
**1.05**  c
**1.06**  true
**1.07**  false
**1.08**  true
**1.09**  true
**1.010**  false
**1.011**  South Dakota
**1.012**  blizzard
**1.013**  Nebraska
**1.014**  Mississippi
**1.015**  cold

# SECTION 2

| | |
|---|---|
| **2.1** | gold |
| **2.2** | lead |
| **2.3** | blades |
| **2.4** | farm |
| **2.5** | Teacher check |
| **2.6** | a |
| **2.7** | c |
| **2.8** | b |
| **2.9** | b |
| **2.10** | a |
| **2.11** | false |
| **2.12** | false |
| **2.13** | true |
| **2.14** | true |

# SELF TEST 2

| | |
|---|---|
| **2.01** | c |
| **2.02** | d |
| **2.03** | a |
| **2.04** | b |
| **2.05** | f |
| **2.06** | e |
| **2.07** | b |
| **2.08** | c |
| **2.09** | a |
| **2.010** | a |
| **2.011** | c |
| **2.012** | b |
| **2.013** | true |
| **2.014** | false |
| **2.015** | true |
| **2.016** | false |
| **2.017** | true |

# SECTION 3

| | |
|---|---|
| **3.1** | Louisiana |
| **3.2** | Missouri |
| **3.3** | 1806 |
| **3.4** | Sacajawea |
| **3.5** | false |
| **3.6** | true |
| **3.7** | false |
| **3.8** | true |
| **3.9** | four |
| **3.10** | South Dakota |
| **3.11** | Gateway Arch |
| **3.12** | St. Louis |
| **3.13** | Teacher check |

# SELF TEST 3

| | |
|---|---|
| **3.01** | c |
| **3.02** | a |
| **3.03** | c |
| **3.04** | b |
| **3.05** | b |
| **3.06** | e |
| **3.07** | a |
| **3.08** | c |
| **3.09** | d |
| **3.010** | true |
| **3.011** | false |
| **3.012** | false |
| **3.013** | true |

## LIFEPAC TEST

1. c
2. b
3. a
4. c
5. b
6. c
7. false
8. true
9. true
10. false
11. false
12. true
13. true
14. false
15. true
16. Missouri
17. Mississippi
18. France
19. Missouri
20. One
21. Corn
22. Kansas
23. gold
24. Iowa
25. Black

## ALTERNATE LIFEPAC TEST

1. true
2. true
3. true
4. false
5. false
6. false
7. true
8. c
9. e
10. f
11. b
12. d
13. a
14. Ozarks
15. gold
16. blades
17. Mississippi
18. Soft
19. Hard
20. Louisiana
21. Missouri
22. tribes
23. buffalo (or bison)
24. Mark Twain
25. Missouri

# HISTORY & GEOGRAPHY 307

## ALTERNATE LIFEPAC TEST

NAME _____

DATE _____

SCORE _____

**Each answer** = 1 point

## Answer *true* or *false*.

1. _____ The Black Hills are sacred to some Native American tribes.

2. _____ A blizzard is a strong Midwestern storm that can shut down schools and roads.

3. _____ Severe thunderstorms can produce tornadoes.

4. _____ Mount Rushmore has the faces of five American presidents.

5. _____ The U.S. government kept all the treaties made with Native Americans.

6. _____ Laura Ingalls Wilder wrote books about her trip with Lewis and Clark.

7. _____ A wind farm is a group of wind turbines.

## Draw a line to the correct answer.

**8.** nomad ●                      **a.** a machine used to harvest crops

**9.** treaty ●                      **b.** a group of people, often soldiers

**10.** reservation ●         **c.** move from place to place

**11.** corps ●                      **d.** a plan of action

**12.** strategy ●                **e.** a peace agreement

**13.** combine ●               **f.** a place set apart for a group of people

## Fill the blank.

**14.** The _____ are the largest mountain range between the Rocky Mountains and the Mississippi River.

**15.** The Black Hills were once home to many _____ mines.

**16.** The _____ of a wind turbine gather the energy from the wind.

**17.** Mark Twain wrote books about life on the _____ River.

**18.** _____ wheat can be made into bread, cake, and cookies.

**19.** _____ wheat can be made into pasta like macaroni.

**20.** Lewis and Clark were sent to explore parts of the region the U.S. bought in the _____ Purchase.

**21.** Lewis and Clark followed the_____ River as they began their journey.

**22.** Sioux, Hidatsa, and Cheyenne are names of Native American _____ .

**23.** Great Plains Native Americans hunted _____ .

**24.** Samuel Clemens was the real name of the writer _____
_____ .

**25.** The longest river in the U.S. is the _____ River.

# HISTORY & GEOGRAPHY 308

Unit 8: Mountain States

# TEACHER NOTES

| MATERIALS NEEDED FOR LESSON | |
|---|---|
| Required | Suggested |
| • LIFEPAC<br>• paper<br>• pencils<br>• crayons | • dictionary<br>• atlas<br>• maps<br>• pictures or videos of the U.S. regions<br>• Internet or encyclopedias |

## INDEPENDENT STUDY ACTIVITY: YOUR STATE OR ANY STATE

As you study the various regions of the U.S., you and your student may find it interesting to study the state in which you live. If you do not live in a U.S. state, your student may choose a state that is of particular interest. In the study, the student will learn about the geography, history, resources, and people of the chosen state. The student should place all of their work in a folder. The student will need an encyclopedia or Internet access in order to complete the study. This activity can be repeated for any state that you find is particularly interesting. It could be a state in which friends or relatives live or a state to which travel is planned. Duplication masters are provided in Unit 301 of this book for the Your State activity and for the Any State activity.

## UNIT REVIEW WORKSHEET:

A duplication master for a review activity is provided for this unit. After the student has completed the unit, have them complete it to prepare for the final LIFEPAC Test.

### » ANSWERS FOR THE REVIEW WORKSHEET

(from left to right by rows)

cowboy, mountain, cactus
cliff dwelling, geyser, potato
railroad, Hoover Dam, Grand Canyon

# ADDITIONAL LEARNING ACTIVITIES

Choose those activities that best suit the needs and interests of your student.

### Section 1: Mountain Geography

1.  Create flash cards for the vocabulary words the student will be learning. On one side of the flash card, the student should write the vocabulary word. On the other side, the student should draw a picture representing the vocabulary word. You may need to help the student decide on an appropriate picture to draw.

2.  Design an experiment so the student understands the effects of the salinity of the Great Salt Lake. There are many available online.

3.  Ask the student to create a diorama showing the rain shadow effect.

4.  Give the student a map of the Rocky Mountains. Have them trace the location of the Continental Divide.

### Section 2: Mountain Resources

1.  Take a potato and monitor as the student cuts it in half. Have the student make a design in the potato so it can be used as a stamp. Make potato stamp art with your student.

2.  Create an experiment where students see how a dam stops the course of a river. You could do this in a sandbox.

3.  Have the student research a U.S. national park in the region.

### Section 3: Mountain Community

1.  Give the student an outline of the western U.S. Ask the student to trace the route of the first transcontinental railroad.

2.  Ask the student to write a letter as if they were a forty-niner during the California gold rush. The letter should explain to a family member on the East Coast their experiences.

3.  Make a meal of food cowboys might have eaten on the trail. If possible, make the meal over a campfire!

### Explore the Internet:

The Internet can be a useful resource for additional activities and information. To show students a film about the construction of the Hoover Dam, visit the PBS website and search "Hoover Dam." Search the key phrase "Idaho Potato Commission for kids" to find interactive games and other activities, and search "Interactive Railroad Project" to play a game about building railroads in the 1800s. Remember to monitor the sites your students visit.

### Administer the LIFEPAC Test.

The test is to be administered in one session. Give no help except with directions.
Evaluate the tests and review areas where the students have done poorly.
Review the pages and activities that stress the concepts tested.
If necessary, administer the Alternate LIFEPAC Test.

## HISTORY & GEOGRAPHY 308: VOWELS FOR MOUNTAIN STATES

For the Mountain states words below, fill in the missing vowels.

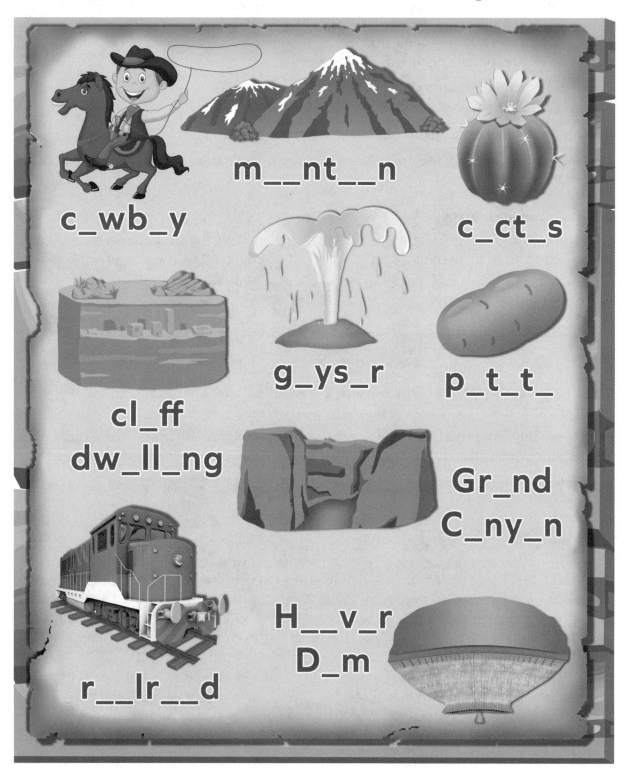

m__nt__n

c_wb_y

c_ct_s

g_ys_r

p_t_t_

cl_ff
dw_ll_ng

Gr_nd
C_ny_n

H__v_r
D_m

r__lr__d

# ANSWER KEYS

## SECTION 1

**1.1**    a.  Helena
        b.  Boise
        c.  Cheyenne
        d.  Carson City
        e.  Salt Lake City
        f.  Denver
        g.  Phoenix
        h.  Santa Fe
**1.2**    Mexico
**1.3**    Montana, Wyoming, Utah, Arizona
**1.4**    Arizona and New Mexico
**1.5**    Colorado River
**1.6**    Great Salt Lake
**1.7**    California
**1.8**    Colorado
**1.9**    Nevada
**1.10**  Colorado
**1.11**  Montana
**1.12**  Pacific Ocean
**1.13**  cactus
**1.14**  Utah
**1.15**  evaporation
**1.16**  Sonoran
**1.17**  false
**1.18**  true
**1.19**  false
**1.20**  false

## SELF TEST 1

**1.01**   c
**1.02**   a
**1.03**   a
**1.04**   c
**1.05**   a
**1.06**   c
**1.07**   false
**1.08**   false
**1.09**   true
**1.010**  true
**1.011**  rain
**1.012**  Evaporation
**1.013**  Arizona
**1.014**  Utah
**1.015**  water

# SECTION 2

| | |
|---|---|
| **2.1** | dam |
| **2.2** | Colorado River |
| **2.3** | Lake Mead |
| **2.4** | Nevada |
| **2.5** | Idaho |
| **2.6** | Teacher check |
| **2.7** | c |
| **2.8** | d |
| **2.9** | d |
| **2.10** | b |
| **2.11** | a |
| **2.12** | false |
| **2.13** | true |
| **2.14** | true |
| **2.15** | false |
| **2.16** | true |

# SELF TEST 2

| | |
|---|---|
| **2.01** | Supreme Court |
| **2.02** | television |
| **2.03** | governor |
| **2.04** | Colorado |
| **2.05** | Pluto |
| **2.06** | Silver |
| **2.07** | a |
| **2.08** | c |
| **2.09** | b |
| **2.010** | c |
| **2.011** | c |
| **2.012** | c |
| **2.013** | f |
| **2.014** | a |
| **2.015** | e |
| **2.016** | d |
| **2.017** | b |

# SECTION 3

| | |
|---|---|
| **3.1** | cliffs |
| **3.2** | Santa Fe |
| **3.3** | Mexico |
| **3.4** | Utah |
| **3.5** | true |
| **3.6** | false |
| **3.7** | false |
| **3.8** | true |
| **3.9** | Colorado |
| **3.10** | Yellowstone |
| **3.11** | geyser |
| **3.12** | Olympics |
| **3.13** | Teacher check |

# SELF TEST 3

| | |
|---|---|
| **3.01** | a |
| **3.02** | c |
| **3.03** | a |
| **3.04** | b |
| **3.05** | b |
| **3.06** | c |
| **3.07** | b |
| **3.08** | false |
| **3.09** | true |
| **3.010** | false |
| **3.011** | true |
| **3.012** | true |
| **3.013** | true |

# LIFEPAC TEST

1. b
2. b
3. c
4. a
5. c
6. b
7. false
8. true
9. false
10. true
11. true
12. false
13. false
14. true
15. true
16. 0 or no
17. cactus
18. Colorado
19. Idaho
20. dam
21. Santa Fe
22. cliff
23. Mexico
24. cook
25. rodeo

# ALTERNATE LIFEPAC TEST

1. true
2. false
3. false
4. false
5. true
6. true
7. false
8. d
9. f
10. e
11. b
12. a
13. c
14. wind
15. cactus
16. governor
17. Hoover
18. Silver
19. Idaho
20. television
21. Colorado
22. Yellowstone
23. Spain
24. rodeo
25. Mexico

# HISTORY & GEOGRAPHY 308

## ALTERNATE LIFEPAC TEST

NAME _____

DATE _____

SCORE _____

**Each answer** = 1 point

**Answer *true* or *false*.**

1. _____ Because there is so much salt in the Great Salt Lake, it is easy for people to float.

2. _____ Wyoming is the most western of the Mountain states.

3. _____ The Continental Divide separates rivers flowing from the Atlantic Ocean from those flowing into the Gulf of Mexico.

4. _____ The Hoover Dam is the largest in the world.

5. _____ Jeannette Rankin voted against the U.S. being involved in World War I and World War II.

6. _____ Old Faithful is the name of a geyser in Yellowstone National Park.

7. _____ A stampede is the name of a cowboy dance.

## Draw a line to the correct answer.

8.  adapt ●
9.  evaporate ●
10. turbine ●
11. pacifist ●
12. dam ●
13. interpreter ●

a.  a structure which stops the flow of water

b.  opposed to violence as a way to solve problems

c.  a person who explains information to another

d.  to change to fit a situation

e.  the machine blades that are turned by water or wind and made into electricity

f.  to change from liquid form to vapor

## Fill in the blank.

14. A rain shadow forms on the side of the mountain from which the _____ doesn't blow.

15. The Saguaro is a type of _____ that can live to be 200 years old.

16. Nellie Tayloe Ross was the first female _____ .

17. Lake Mead is a reservoir located behind the _____ Dam.

18. _____ is used in making photographs and mirrors.

19. _____ produces 1/3 of the potatoes grown in the U.S.

20. Philo T. Farnsworth invented the electric _____ .

21. The _____ River flows through the Grand Canyon.

22. _____ was the first U.S. national park.

23. Coronado was an explorer from _____ who traveled to Mexico and the southwestern U.S.

24. A _____ was held at the end of a cattle drive to show off the cowboys' skills.

25. The war between _____ and the U.S. ended with the Treaty of Guadalupe-Hidalgo.

# HISTORY & GEOGRAPHY 309

Unit 9: Pacific States

# TEACHER NOTES

| MATERIALS NEEDED FOR LESSON | |
|---|---|
| Required | Suggested |
| • LIFEPAC<br>• paper<br>• pencils<br>• crayons | • dictionary<br>• atlas<br>• maps<br>• pictures or videos of the U.S. regions<br>• Internet or encyclopedias |

## INDEPENDENT STUDY ACTIVITY: YOUR STATE OR ANY STATE

As you study the various regions of the U.S., you and your student may find it interesting to study the state in which you live. If you do not live in a U.S. state, your student may choose a state that is of particular interest. In the study, the student will learn about the geography, history, resources, and people of the chosen state. The student should place all of their work in a folder. The student will need an encyclopedia or Internet access in order to complete the study. This activity can be repeated for any state that you find is particularly interesting. It could be a state in which friends or relatives live or a state to which travel is planned. Duplication masters are provided in Unit 301 of this book for the Your State activity and for the Any State activity.

## UNIT REVIEW WORKSHEET:

A duplication master for a review activity is provided for this unit. After the student has completed the unit, have them complete it to prepare for the final LIFEPAC Test.

### » ANSWERS FOR THE REVIEW WORKSHEET

1. volcano
2. Washington
3. California
4. Klondike
5. Hawaii
6. Iditarod
7. Yosemite
8. Silicon
9. Alaska
10. Leprosy
11. commercial
12. Oregon

# ADDITIONAL LEARNING ACTIVITIES

Choose those activities that best suit the needs and interests of your student.

## Section 1: Pacific Geography

1. Create flash cards for the vocabulary words the student will be learning. On one side of the flash card, the student should write the vocabulary word. On the other side, the student should draw a picture representing the vocabulary word. You may need to help the student decide on an appropriate picture to draw.

2. Have the student create a water color picture of the night sky on an evening when the aurora borealis is present.

3. Help the student to graph the average monthly temperature of Anchorage, Alaska, and Honolulu, Hawaii. Compare the differences in temperature.

4. As a science project, create a volcano with your student using baking soda and other ingredients.

## Section 2: Pacific Resources

1. Discuss the work of Father Damien. With your student, participate in a service project for your community.

2. Have your student participate in a flight simulator game. The student may get a sense of challenges faced when flying an aircraft. There are many video games on the web or that can be borrowed from a library.

3. Eat some of the fruit that is grown in California, Washington, and Hawaii.
   For example, serve strawberries, apples, and pineapple.

## Section 3: Pacific Community

1. Direct your student in researching the Iditarod race. Have them research the training needed for the race, the supplies needed, or the challenging route taken.

2. Ask the student to research the highest mountain on each continent. Have the student compare the mountain heights to see how Denali in North America compares.

3. Direct the student in drawing a picture of a beautiful Hawaiian scene.

### Explore the Internet:

The Internet can be a useful resource for additional activities and information. Visit the Discovery Kids website and search "volcano" to play an interactive game about volcanoes. Search the key word "Iditarod" to find websites with information about this famous dog sled race. Remember to monitor the sites your students visit.

### Administer the LIFEPAC Test.

The test is to be administered in one session. Give no help except with directions. Evaluate the tests and review areas where the students have done poorly. Review the pages and activities that stress the concepts tested. If necessary, administer the Alternate LIFEPAC Test.

# HISTORY & GEOGRAPHY 309:
# PACIFIC STATES CROSSWORD PUZZLE REVIEW

Alaska
California
commercial
Hawaii
Iditarod
Klondike
leprosy
Oregon
Silicon
volcano
Washington
Yosemite

## ACROSS

3. The hottest temperature recorded in the U.S. was in Death Valley in this state.
4. The gold rush in Alaska was also known by this name.
5. A series of islands make up this state.
8. The valley in California where many computers are made and designed is known as this.
9. Denali, the highest mountain in North America, is located in this state.

10. Father Damien was a priest who worked with people with Hansen's disease also known as this.
11. The Boeing Company is the second-largest producer of this kind of airplane.
12. Crater Lake National Park is located in this state.

## DOWN

1. Mt. St. Helens is the name of this.
2. This state produces more apples than any other state.
6. A famous dog sled race in Alaska is known as this.

7. This national park in California is home to the rock formation known as Half Dome.

# ANSWER KEYS

## SECTION 1

**1.1**   a.  Olympia
       b.  Salem
       c.  Sacramento
       d.  Juneau
       e.  Honolulu
**1.2**   120 degrees west
**1.3**   California
**1.4**   Washington
**1.5**   Columbia River
**1.6**   Hawaii
**1.7**   Canada
**1.8**   Arctic Ocean
**1.9**   Pacific Ocean
**1.10**  Mexico
**1.11**  Alaska
**1.12**  earthquakes
**1.13**  volcanoes
**1.14**  Richter
**1.15**  California
**1.16**  true
**1.17**  false
**1.18**  true
**1.19**  false

## SELF TEST 1

**1.01**   a
**1.02**   c
**1.03**   c
**1.04**   b
**1.05**   b
**1.06**   true
**1.07**   true
**1.08**   false
**1.09**   false
**1.010** false
**1.011** Oregon
**1.012** Alaska
**1.013** California
**1.014** lava
**1.015** Mt. St. Helens

# SECTION 2

| | |
|---|---|
| **2.1** | Washington |
| **2.2** | Apple |
| **2.3** | medicine |
| **2.4** | California |
| **2.5** | true |
| **2.6** | false |
| **2.7** | true |
| **2.8** | true |
| **2.9** | d |
| **2.10** | b |
| **2.11** | e |
| **2.12** | a |
| **2.13** | c |

# SELF TEST 2

| | |
|---|---|
| **2.01** | d |
| **2.02** | e |
| **2.03** | b |
| **2.04** | a |
| **2.05** | c |
| **2.06** | b |
| **2.07** | a |
| **2.08** | c |
| **2.09** | a |
| **2.010** | c |
| **2.011** | b |
| **2.012** | c |
| **2.013** | true |
| **2.014** | false |
| **2.015** | true |
| **2.016** | false |
| **2.017** | false |

# SECTION 3

| | |
|---|---|
| **3.1** | true |
| **3.2** | false |
| **3.3** | false |
| **3.4** | true |
| **3.5** | Teacher check |
| **3.6** | California |
| **3.7** | Washington |
| **3.8** | Apple |
| **3.9** | 1993 |
| **3.10** | a |
| **3.11** | c |
| **3.12** | d |
| **3.13** | c |
| **3.14** | Teacher check |

# SELF TEST 3

| | |
|---|---|
| **3.01** | b |
| **3.02** | b |
| **3.03** | a |
| **3.04** | c |
| **3.05** | a |
| **3.06** | b |
| **3.07** | a |
| **3.08** | false |
| **3.09** | true |
| **3.010** | true |
| **3.011** | false |
| **3.012** | true |
| **3.013** | false |

# LIFEPAC TEST

1. b
2. a
3. c
4. b
5. b
6. c
7. false
8. true
9. true
10. true
11. false
12. false
13. true
14. false
15. true
16. northern
17. Pacific
18. Disney
19. wing
20. Cleary
21. Damien
22. Hawaii
23. Alaska
24. Apple
25. Washington

# ALTERNATE LIFEPAC TEST

1. false
2. true
3. false
4. true
5. false
6. true
7. true
8. d
9. e
10. a
11. f
12. c
13. b
14. California
15. Sacramento
16. Hawaii
17. Obama
18. Washington
19. 2
20. apples
21. Alaska
22. Silicon
23. Alaska
24. Yosemite
25. Crater Lake

# HISTORY & GEOGRAPHY 309

## ALTERNATE LIFEPAC TEST

NAME _____

DATE _____

SCORE _____

**Each answer** = 1 point

## Answer *true* or *false.*

1. _____ The Richter scale measures the strength of a hurricane.

2. _____ The Arctic Ocean is north of Alaska.

3. _____ The capital of Oregon is Sacramento.

4. _____ Walt Disney created the character Mickey Mouse.

5. _____ The 50th U.S. state was Alaska.

6. _____ The explorer James Cook named Hawaii the Sandwich Islands.

7. _____ The Golden Gate Bridge was the world's longest suspension bridge in 1937.

## Draw a line to the correct answer.

8. silicon ●

9. magma ●

10. dormant ●

11. lava ●

12. installed ●

13. reservation ●

**a.** not active

**b.** make plans at a hotel or restaurant

**c.** to put in

**d.** a material used in making computers

**e.** hot volcanic material <u>under</u> the Earth's surface

**f.** hot volcanic material when it reaches the Earth's surface

## Fill in the blank.

14. The San Andreas Fault is located in the state of _____ .

15. The capital of California is _____ .

16. Father Damien worked with lepers who lived in the state of _____ .

17. U.S. presidents from the Pacific states include Nixon, Reagan, and _____ .

18. The Boeing company is located in the state of _____ .

19. The Boeing company is the number _____ producer of commercial airplanes in the world.

20. Washington is the leading grower of _____ .

21. The Klondike gold rush took place in _____ .

22. The _____ Valley is home to many computer companies.

23. The Iditarod race takes place in the state of _____ .

24. Half Dome and Bridalveil Fall are located in _____ National Park.

25. _____ is the deepest lake in the U.S.

# HISTORY & GEOGRAPHY 310

Unit 10: U.S. Geography & History Review

# TEACHER NOTES

| MATERIALS NEEDED FOR LESSON | |
|---|---|
| Required | Suggested |
| • LIFEPAC<br>• paper<br>• pencils<br>• crayons | • dictionary<br>• atlas<br>• maps<br>• pictures or videos of the U.S. regions<br>• Internet or encyclopedias |

## INDEPENDENT STUDY ACTIVITY: YOUR STATE OR ANY STATE

As you study the various regions of the U.S., you and your student may find it interesting to study the state in which you live. If you do not live in a U.S. state, your student may choose a state that is of particular interest. In the study, the student will learn about the geography, history, resources, and people of the chosen state. The student should place all of their work in a folder. The student will need an encyclopedia or Internet access in order to complete the study. This activity can be repeated for any state that you find is particularly interesting. It could be a state in which friends or relatives live or a state to which travel is planned. Duplication masters are provided in Unit 301 of this book for the Your State activity and for the Any State activity.

## UNIT REVIEW WORKSHEET:

A duplication master for a review activity is provided for this unit. After the student has completed the unit, have them complete it to prepare for the final LIFEPAC Test.

### » ANSWERS FOR THE REVIEW WORKSHEET

**E**   The Pilgrims settled in Massachusetts.

**E**   The Everglades became a U.S. national park.

**W**   Texas became a country and then a state.

**E**   French fur trappers explored the region of the Great Lakes.

**W**   The Hoover Dam was built.

**E**   The Revolutionary War was fought.

**W**   The volcano Mt. St. Helens erupted in Washington.

**W**   Queen Liliuokalani was the last ruler of Hawaii.

**W**   Settlers flocked to California and Alaska during the gold rushes.

**E**   George Washington served as the first president of the United States.

**Administer the LIFEPAC Test.**

# GEOGRAPHY & HISTORY 310 REVIEW: EAST AND WEST
## U.S. REVIEW

**Identify if the following events happened on the east or west side of the Mississippi River.**

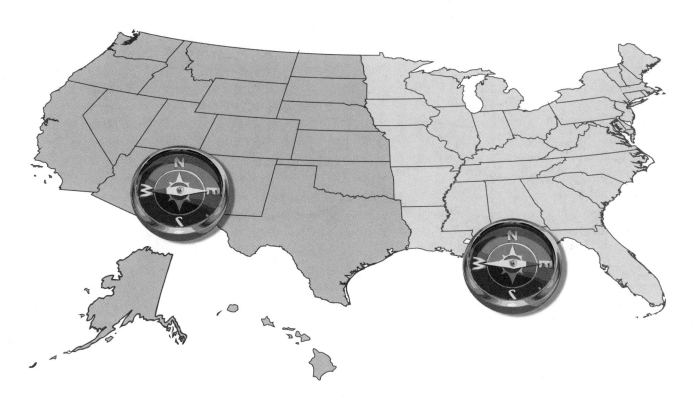

- [ ] The Pilgrims settled in Massachusetts.
- [ ] The Everglades became a U.S. national park.
- [ ] Texas became a country and then a state.
- [ ] French fur trappers explored the region of the Great Lakes.
- [ ] The Hoover Dam was built.
- [ ] The Revolutionary War was fought.
- [ ] The volcano Mt. St. Helens erupted in Washington.
- [ ] Queen Liliuokalani was the last ruler of Hawaii.
- [ ] Settlers flocked to California and Alaska during the gold rushes.
- [ ] George Washington served as the first president of the United States.

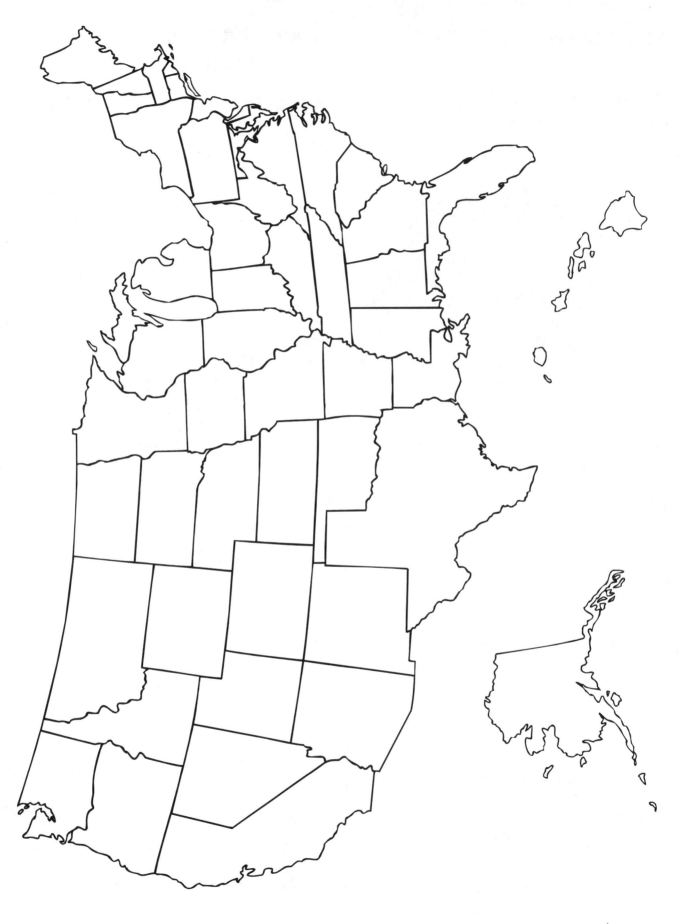

# ADDITIONAL LEARNING ACTIVITIES

Choose those activities that best suit the needs and interests of your student.

### Section 1: U.S. Geography

1. If the student has created flash cards for all of the vocabulary words for the LIFEPACs, quiz them using the cards.

2. Give the student a blank map of the U.S. and have them fill in the main geographical features.

3. Take Play-Doh® or modeling clay and have the student choose to create one state out of the material.

### Section 2: Eastern U.S. Review

1. Give the student a blank map of the U.S. Have them locate five important cities located along the eastern side of the Mississippi River.

2. Give the student a blank map of the U.S. Have the student color the map illustrating when different parts of the country became part of the United States. For example, have the student shade in the Louisiana Purchase and label the date it took place.

3. Ask the student to create a poster which illustrates the main geographical features of the eastern U.S.

### Section 3: Western U.S. Review

1. Give the student a blank map of the U.S. Have them locate five important cities located along the Pacific Ocean.

2. Have the student make a Venn diagram in which they compare and contrast the eastern and western U.S.

3. Ask the student to create a poster which illustrates the main geographical features of the western U.S.

### Explore the Internet:

The Internet can be a useful resource for additional activities and information.
Search "Scholastic map games" to find activities that test map skills.
Visit the History Channel website and type "games" in the site search box to find a variety of interactive history games. Remember to monitor the sites your students visit.

# ANSWER KEYS

## SECTION 1

**1.1**    a.  a red circle

         b.  a red star

**1.2**    Florida, Louisiana, and Texas

**1.3**    North Dakota, South Dakota, Nebraska, Kansas, Oklahoma, and Texas

**1.4**    Utah

**1.5**    Lake Huron

**1.6**    The Atlantic Ocean

**1.7**    The Gulf of Mexico

**1.8**    Canada

**1.9**    Mexico

**1.10**    Pacific Ocean

**1.11**    Arctic Ocean

**1.12**    Appalachian Mountains

**1.13**    Long Island

**1.14**    The Chesapeake Bay

**1.15**    The Ohio River

**1.16**    Outer Banks

**1.17**    Lakes Huron, Michigan, Ontario, Superior, and Erie

**1.18**    Lake Okeechobee

**1.19**    Wisconsin, Illinois, Kentucky, Tennessee, and Mississippi

**1.20**    Augusta, Maine and Montpelier, Vermont

**1.21**    The White Mountains

**1.22**    The Gulf of Mexico

**1.23**    The Rocky Mountains

**1.24**    Minnesota, Iowa, Missouri, Arkansas, and Louisiana

**1.25**    Alaska

**1.26**    Hawaii

**1.27**    The Rio Grande

**1.28**    The Great Salt Lake

**1.29**    Pacific Ocean, Arctic Ocean, Gulf of Alaska

**1.30**    The Missouri River

**1.31**    The Colorado River

**1.32**    Denali

**1.33**    The Columbia River

## SELF TEST 1

**1.01**    b

**1.02**    b

**1.03**    c

**1.04**    a

**1.05**    c

**1.06**    false

**1.07**    true

**1.08**    false

**1.09**    false

**1.010**  true

**1.011**  Washington D.C.

**1.012**  Arctic

**1.013**  Gulf of Mexico

**1.014**  Pacific

**1.015**  Colorado

# SECTION 2

**2.1** Revolutionary
**2.2** democracy
**2.3** Harvard
**2.4** New York City
**2.5** Pilgrims
**2.6** true
**2.7** false
**2.8** false
**2.9** true
**2.10** true
**2.11** France
**2.12** Civil
**2.13** governor
**2.14** bayous
**2.15** Mississippi

# SELF TEST 2

**2.01** d
**2.02** c
**2.03** e
**2.04** f
**2.05** b
**2.06** a
**2.07** b
**2.08** b
**2.09** a
**2.010** c
**2.011** c
**2.012** b
**2.013** true
**2.014** false
**2.015** true
**2.016** true
**2.017** false
**2.018** false

# SECTION 3

| | |
|---|---|
| **3.1** | false |
| **3.2** | false |
| **3.3** | true |
| **3.4** | true |
| **3.5** | false |
| **3.6** | false |
| **3.7** | false |
| **3.8** | false |
| **3.9** | true |
| **3.10** | true |
| **3.11** | earthquakes |
| **3.12** | volcanoes |
| **3.13** | Washington |
| **3.14** | California |
| **3.15** | commercial airplanes |

# SELF TEST 3

| | |
|---|---|
| **3.01** | b |
| **3.02** | c |
| **3.03** | a |
| **3.04** | c |
| **3.05** | a |
| **3.06** | Henry Ford |
| **3.07** | Hawaii |
| **3.08** | computer |
| **3.09** | Abraham Lincoln |
| **3.010** | Washington |
| **3.011** | true |
| **3.012** | false |
| **3.013** | true |
| **3.014** | false |
| **3.015** | false |

# LIFEPAC TEST

1. c
2. a
3. c
4. b
5. c
6. b
7. b
8. c
9. false
10. true
11. false
12. false
13. true
14. false
15. true
16. false
17. true
18. true
19. Texas
20. Missouri
21. Rocky
22. Hawaii
23. Florida
24. gold
25. airplanes

# ALTERNATE LIFEPAC TEST

1. false
2. true
3. false
4. false
5. false
6. true
7. false
8. c
9. d
10. e
11. a
12. b
13. Washington, D.C.
14. Pacific
15. Mississippi
16. Pilgrims
17. Florida
18. Texas
19. Louisiana
20. England
21. Atlantic
22. airplane
23. California
24. gold
25. computer

# HISTORY & GEOGRAPHY 310

## ALTERNATE LIFEPAC TEST

**NAME** _____

**DATE** _____

**SCORE** _____

**Each answer** = 1 point

## Answer *true* or *false*.

1. _____ The Appalachian Mountains run along the west coast of the U.S.

2. _____ Denali is located in the state of Alaska.

3. _____ The Rio Grande River forms the border between the U.S. and Canada.

4. _____ The Civil Rights movement brought an end to slavery.

5. _____ Lake Michigan is not one of the Great Lakes.

6. _____ Hawaii was the last state to join the U.S.

7. _____ Mount St. Helens is the tallest mountain in the U.S.

## Draw a line to the correct answer.

8.  Founded the Jamestown Colony   •

9.  U.S. president during the Civil War   •

10. Worked in the auto industry   •

11. First president of the U.S.   •

12. Served as a president, governor, and senator   •

a. George Washington

b. Sam Houston

c. John Smith

d. Abraham Lincoln

e. Henry Ford

## Fill in the blank.

13. _____ is the capital of the United States.

14. Hawaii is located within the _____ Ocean.

15. The _____ River runs south from Minnesota to Louisiana.

16. _____ first settled in what is now Massachusetts.

17. The U.S. space program is headquartered in Cape Canaveral, _____ .

18. _____ was a country after gaining its freedom from Mexico before becoming a state.

19. The _____ Purchase gave the U.S. much of the land west of the Mississippi River.

20. The Revolutionary War gave the U.S. colonies freedom from _____ .

21. The St. Lawrence Seaway connects the Great Lakes with the _____ Ocean.

22. The Wright brothers built the first _____ .

23. _____ is the leading producer of strawberries in the U.S.

24. The Alaskan _____ rush brought many settlers to the state.

25. Silicon Valley in California is the center of the _____ industry.